A PRICE ON MY

KEVIN CALLAGHAN was born in Crumpsall, Manchester, on 1st March 1944, the elder son of Jim and Renee Callaghan, well-known figures in the licensing trade in the area. After leaving Grange St. School, where he was known as "a delicate little lad in glasses" he spent more than 22 years in the Royal Army Ordnance Corps, rising to the rank of Warrant Officer Class One. He served in Germany, Bahrain, Northern Ireland and the Falkland Islands and is the only man to have been awarded the George Medal and Queen's Gallantry Medal.

While 16 of his colleagues were killed in Northern Ireland, Callaghan, during two tours there, defused 27 bombs, containing thousands of pounds of explosives and dealt with many more suspect devices. He and Valerie have a son, David, and daughter, Samantha. Kevin still serves the Army as a Major in the TA and lives in the North of England.

TERRY GORRY has worked on the sports desk of the *Manchester Evening News* for nearly 30 years and has also travelled extensively for the paper as an Army features writer.

A PRICE ON MY HEAD

by
Kevin Callaghan GM, QGM
with Terry Gorry

OWL
BOOKS

First published November 1993
by
Owl Books
P.O. Box 60
Wigan WN1 2QB.

ISBN 1 873888 50 3

Designed and produced by Coveropen Ltd., Wigan.

Text produced via high resolution DTP in ITC Bookman 11.5/13.5pt.

Printed and bound in Great Britain.

CONTENTS

For my family, who waited,
and for all with whom I served.

ACKNOWLEDGEMENTS

My sincere thanks are due to the members of 321 EOD Section Northern Ireland, for their support on operations and to Terry Gorry, without whom this book would not have been possible.

INTRODUCTION

KEVIN Callaghan joined the Army aged $17^1/2$ with his sole ambition to drive big trucks — and was disowned by his father for doing so. Several years later his father watched proudly as Kevin, all 5 ft. 4 ins. of him, was decorated for the second time by the Queen to become his country's most decorated peacetime soldier. To this day he remains the only man to be awarded the George Medal and the Queen's Gallantry Medal. Those medals were earned the hard way. Far from driving big trucks, Callaghan became one of the Army's most respected bomb disposal operators in an age when the terrorists were becoming ever more knowledgeable and their booby-traps increasingly ingenious. It led to him, in Army folklore, having a bounty of £10,000 put on his head by the IRA, who came within a hairsbreadth of collecting their evil payoff as the little man from Manchester took them on in a deadly, sinister game of life and death.

CHAPTER 1

Somebody's Trying To Kill Me

THE thudding noise in my ears stopped me in my tracks. What on earth was it, I asked myself as I paused to listen. It was disrupting my train of thought as I carefully weighed the most vital decision of my life.

Suddenly, I realised where the noise was coming from: it was my heart! It was pounding away as I pondered a decision that, within the next few seconds, would determine whether I lived or died.

The noise of my ticker going hell for leather was magnified, because I was wearing a tight-fitting helmet. It was part of the heavily-armoured bomb suit in which I was clad as I stared, pulse racing, at a device just a few inches in front of me, which had been left courtesy of the IRA, and which, I had just realised, had been booby-trapped with the sole intention of killing me.

The device, a blast incendiary, was a one-gallon can of petrol, to which was attached a mortar bomb, a home-made detonator and a timing and power unit. It was sitting behind the driver's seat of a hijacked fuel tanker. A fairly routine set-up in Northern Ireland. What gave it an added degree of difficulty and horror was the wicked little device that had been attached to it and which I had spotted in the nick of time.

As a British Army bomb disposal operator—or "Felix"—it was down to me and me alone, to tackle it and on my actions in the next second or so depended, quite simply, my life.

Either I beat the bomb or it would incinerate me as the petrol ignited in a fireball at a rate of 4,500 metres per second.

As I pondered my fateful decision I did not have time to reflect on the fact that somebody was trying to kill me...

CHAPTER 2

Latch-key Kid

LIFE in Northern Ireland had its compensations after all, I had thought, some time earlier, as I returned to a wave of congratulation and acclaim after foiling another IRA bomb attempt. The adrenalin was still flowing and I made the most of one of the most enjoyable aspects of the teamwork and camaraderie that existed within the close-knit ranks of one of the Army's highly-specialised units, which was part of my life.

I felt very much a part of this family of unique men. And for me, this was an entirely different environment to the one in which I had spent my early years as an outcast in the backstreets of Manchester.

Whenever I thought back twenty five or more years to my days in one of the less salubrious areas of the city, it was to reflect that I had certainly come a long way from the time when I was a little guy in glasses, who nobody wanted to know.

The fact that I was something of an outcast was not really due to the fact that the street kids where I lived were any crueller than youngsters the world over; Northerners, of course, are renowned for their innate friendliness. I was just a victim of circumstances.

Almost from the moment I was born in Crumpsall Hospital on March 1st 1944, missing being a Leap Year baby by one day, I was wrapped in cotton wool. The Irish nurse who handed me to my mother remarked at the time: "Ooh, you've got a lovely Kevin there!" It was the name I was given as a result, which is how I ended up with an Irish name.

Lovely Kevin I might have been, but it was not long before those in the know pronounced me "delicate".

My early years in Chatham Street, not far from Greymare Lane Market and in the shadow of the local pit, were spent being treated for fluid on the lungs and, just for good measure, a mastoid.

While my Dad was away serving in the Merchant Navy, Mum was taking me on daily trips to hospital, where I had numerous tests and a series of injections. I was very weak and as a result was not allowed to do anything of a robust physical nature of the sort that kids love to do as a normal part of growing up. By the time I was old enough to go to school I was well enough to be able to attend Bradford Memorial Infants School, but the "weak" tag was still firmly attached to me and any sort of sports activity was definitely ruled out.

Consequently, I was the one who always stood and watched while the rest of the schoolkids enjoyed themselves in the rough and tumble of their various games. I was not exactly shunned, but I was always the outsider.

My early school years were spent with very few friends, because while they were all out running about, I was taking it easy. There was always a kid who would be leader, who everybody wanted to be with, but even when I tried I was not allowed to join in and be "one of the gang" because I was marked down as "different".

This sad fact of life has had an effect on me that I have brought with me into later life; not being allowed to play the normal ball sports left me with no sporting interest whatsoever, and as a result I have never kicked a ball about or run round the garden with my children. That is very sad, but it is something that never occurred to me.

One of the better consequences of my enforced loneliness in early life, however, is that now I am quite happy with my own company from time to time. Solitude is something that comes easily to me, although I do enjoy meeting people.

As time went on, I inherited two more handicaps, that put a strain on my somewhat non-existent social life. I was beginning to realise that I was never going to be a big lad, as the other kids at school began to outgrow me — and then there was my brother, Paul.

Paul was seven years younger than I was and it was not long before I was put in charge of him. Wherever I went I had to drag him around with me, so it became doubly difficult to make friends or join in a gang because I was now noticed as the little kid who always brought his kid brother along.

The times when I could get out to mix with the other kids were limited anyway, because I had become a "latch-key kid" and had a string of other duties to perform.

Mum worked for a raincoat manufacturer in Ancoats, while my dad, who had now left the navy, had a variety of jobs. Ours was a decidedly working-class environment and it was my task to come home from school, get the key from a neighbour and do a string of chores. I was not allowed to light the fire, but it had to be laid, the potatoes had to be peeled and if I had not done these and one hundred and one other tasks allotted me by the time my parents got home I was in trouble! Needless to say, I didn't think a great deal of this arrangement as it meant I could rarely go out.

For a long, long time, I lived in fear of my father. He was very strict and if he said "No" he meant it and I received many a clout for usurping his authority — probably well deserved. My parents were tough on me, but it was just a result of the circumstances in which we lived and they both worked extremely hard.

When Dad left the Merchant Navy he went, at first, to work with my uncle, repairing and maintaining fridges for Frigidaire, but then he got a job at Tip-top Bakeries which meant he left home at an exceedingly early hour, came home in the afternoon to have a nap, before going out in the evening waiting on tables in the local pub to make ends meet.

Consequently, it was quite normal to expect me to play my part in this hard-working environment. Another of my tasks was to clean Dad's shoes on a Saturday, but this was a chore that brought an immediate reward, because for doing so I received my weekly pocket money of half a crown — or twelve and a half pence as it would be now.

Saturdays, in fact, gave me an early insight into the commercial aspect of doing work for others; there was the shoe-cleaning for my half dollar. And then there was the weekly chicken run. Every Saturday I used to go shopping for the ladies in our street at Greymare Lane Market.

It was my task to take their orders for chicken, which was quite a luxury item in those days, but a bargain one, price-wise. I got to know the lady who ran the stall quite well, but I could never understand how she could bear to cut the heads off the birds, gut them and throw all the guts in a large dustbin. I stood there heaving while she prepared six to ten chickens for me in this way — but it was well worth it when I dutifully delivered them to my ladies and received tips from them which augmented my two and six quite nicely.

One of the more enjoyable aspects of my early life was a visit to the great liner, Queen Mary. Only trouble was — I was too young to be able to appreciate it!

My father had a job on the great Cunarder as a sick

berth attendant and Mum and I spent some time on board, being able to stay with him. I even had a chap who was assigned especially to me. He slept outside the cabin door to protect me and it must all have been terribly grand. Or so they tell me. I was too young to be able to remember it.

There was another drawback that began to hamper me as I grew — if that's the right word — towards my teens. I was never clever at school and there were a number of things I simply did not understand. But it was only when it became time for me to go to Grange Street Secondary School on the other side of the main road that all suddenly became clear — literally.

It was realised that I could not see properly and needed glasses. Off I went for my eye test at the optician's at the top of Geymare Lane where I was duly fitted out with specs.

I stepped out of the shop — and into a whole new world! I stared in disbelief at a clock I had looked at for years and realised it had a series of black lines in a pattern on its face, which previously I had seen only as a white face with black fingers and numbers. It was quite incredible and I will always remember the sensation of amazement at what I had been missing. So now, I was not only the little kid who always had his brother tagging along. To those with a crueller sense of fun I was, now "Speccy Cally". But at least I could see what was going on and life was about to take a turn for the better.

My parents moved into the club catering business and we upped and left Chatham Street and moved to the British Rail Staff Association Club at Ancoats where Mum and Dad had got the job as steward and stewardess.

This was more like it! At last I began to enjoy life. There was plenty of activity at night, I learned all about running the club, taking care of the cellar and doing the bar work.

This was a completely new scene and taught me the rudiments of running a licensed premises.

Soon I was into my last year at school, which I spent going from the club to Grange Street on a pushbike. Then it became time to step out into the world on my own and find a job.

This was not too difficult as my father put in a word for me at Tip-Top Bakery, which was one of the places he had worked after leaving the Navy. I left school on a Friday and began work on Monday as a van boy, for which I earned £15 for a 40-hour week.

It was not a bad start, if nothing special, despite the very early starting times. By the time I was sixteen however, I was beginning to realise it was not for me, but I pressed on for another six months, encouraged now that life had taken an upswing with the arrival in my life of an extremely important piece of machinery: my first motor bike. It was a Triumph Tiger Cub, packing a whole 199cc, which I bought second hand with £100 my Dad lent me, interest free. Life was beginning to take off as I went from immobile to mobile in a flash.

But soon after I got into the bike scene and passed my test I began to fancy something a bit more powerful, which duly arrived in the shape of a BSA Gold Flash — 650 cc this time. Just before Christmas, however, after eighteen months at work, the bike and I parted company at a roundabout.

I attempted to go round the island too fast, hit it instead and came off, escaping with a wrenched foot and a damaged shin. I had got off lightly, no doubt about it. But it meant a spell off work and during the time I was laid up I started doing more work for my father until, in the end, I handed in my notice at the bakery and started work for him full-time.

There was a great deal of new-found freedom now, but

life was not without its drawbacks, because the problem of working for family is that, while you are paid a proper wage, people do tend to take advantage of you.

Soon, it became a regular case of: "Kevin, can you go and open up tonight?" or "Can you do so and so?" until, eventually, I seemed to be doing everything and was left with no spare time.

Mind you, financially, I now had few worries. Dad paid me well. I was allowed to keep the profis on the catering, which consisted basically of hot dogs, sausage and chicken rolls and suchlike and I did quite nicely out of this: around £20. 5s a week, which was a fair old wage for a teenager in those days. And it was thanks to this new-found wealth that I took another important step up the social scale with the purchase of a second-hand van, an Austin A40, whose registration number, OMA 222 I remember so well.

But by now I had learned the hard lesson that money is not everything. What good is a car — or van — if the only time you can use it is when everybody else is at work and when you are working everybody else is on their leisure time?

The reason I now had the van was to become one of the most significant influences in my life. I had just met a lovely girl called Valerie, with whom I was very taken. Sensible girl that she was, she simply refused to ride on the back of my bike, so I knew at once: I had to make an immediate change of plan. I had to get rid of the bike and get a car.

Dad taxed and insured it for me in his name, as you could do in those days. I was about to pass my test and with another interest free loan from him I was away!

This was most important to me. I had decided I had to hang on to this rather special girl, who I had met by chance in a coffee bar.

Fate took a romantic hand one night when I was playing the fruit machine in a place called the '700' in Levenshulme, where the building still survives.

Upstairs was a licensed bar, but as I was only seventeen I was not allowed up there, so it was the prospect of getting the three lemons up on the machine which stood at the foot of the stairs that was occupying my thoughts when they were interrupted by a voice saying: "Kev, Valerie wants to pass".

I looked up and it was a lad known as Jackie the Nice, who worked there, who was trying to attract my attention. Jackie was as queer as a nine-bob note, there was no doubt about that, but he certainly did me a favour that night because the Vision to whom he was referring simply took my breath away!

"Do you know Valerie?" asked Jackie as she made to get past and up the stairs to the bar.

"No. But I wish I did!" I replied, quick as a flash. Anxious not to allow the Vision to escape, I tried all the usual chat-up lines on her: "Where do you live? Where do you work? And so on.

I learned that she came from Bramhall, and as we had now moved to the British Rail club in Edgeley, Stockport, this was quite near my home, I realised.

She was trying to extricate herself from my company and escape, but as she was going up the stairs I called after her: "Well, when are you taking me out then?"

"Well, I'm not taking **you** out" she replied and disappeared into the bar; out of my clutches as I was not allowed to follow her in there.

But I was smitten and I was not going to be put off easily and when she came downstairs to visit the loo she found me lying in ambush.

"Well, how about me taking you out next Wednesday

then?" I said cheekily. To my amazement, back came the answer: "Yes, all right".

I could not believe it! She was clearly way out of my league and I honestly believed I was being patronised. But, patronised or not, I pressed on anyway and we set up a date for the following week, agreeing to meet on the corner outside the Manchester cinema where "Spartacus" was showing.

The lads in the coffee bar were unanimous: "She won't turn up" they agreed. I didn't think she would either, but come the appointed evening I was stood on the corner in good time, dressed in my best bib and tucker, with not a hair out of place on the off chance that I was wrong.

"She's not going to come. She's not going to come" I kept repeating to myself, feeling more and more miserable. Wrong! Suddenly, I got the thrill of my life when I saw her approaching.

"Hello" she smiled and made my day. Off we went to see Kirk Douglas hacking his way through history, then I walked her to the bus that took her back to Bramhall. And Kevin Callaghan was, at that precise moment, the world's happiest fella. Especially as she had agreed to see me again!

But Valerie would not see me AND the bike, so, I decided there was only one thing for it. I had to swap it for four wheels. My new mode of transport met with her approval and my driving was also approved by the examiner, who passed me for my licence at the first time of asking.

I was now happy in my social life, but work was a different matter and I was becoming increasingly unhappy with my lot.

It had become my burning ambition to drive big trucks; little man, big truck, so to speak, but that was not going to happen if I stayed where I was. So, it was at this time that the idea of joining the services occurred to me, though I never mentioned it at home.

Nor did I mention where I was off to when I walked into the Manchester recruiting office and announced: "I want to drive".

"Right. RAOC for you" they told me. It was all the encouragement I needed and without further ado I signed on the dotted line for twenty two years, without the slightest inkling of the radical changes that were about to take place in my life during the ensuing few years.

CHAPTER 3

The Queen Has Gained A Soldier

LITTLE did I suspect the furore my announcement that I would be leaving home in six weeks and going into the Army would cause.

There was hell on! It was a terrific family upset when I walked in from the recruiting office and made my announcement. The upshot of it was that my father practically disowned me on the spot with the words:

"The Queen has gained a soldier, but I have lost a son".

That was it. I hadn't expected him to take my news so much to heart. It made me extremely unhappy that we did not speak from then on except for the bare necessities and it was a good many years before our relationship became friendly again and he was able to accept the situation.

But my mind was made up, I had signed on, so off I went to Blackdown Barracks in Hampshire for basic training. This was extremely hard at first, lots of spit and polish and verbal abuse as the instructors knocked us into shape with their usual "character building" process.

The pay was a mere fiver a week or so — quite a come-down from the plutocratic existence I had become used to and I began to think: "My God. What have I done?"

But the rough and tough slog of basic training does not last forever. It only seems as if it does! Within thirteen weeks I was being sent to Munchen Gladbach, West Germany for my first tour abroad and basic driver training.

Now, I was doing more or less what I wanted to do. I began to thoroughly enjoy the ife and quickly went from B 3 Grade Driver, to B 2, learning to handle and maintain various vehicles.

But when I was sent to join my unit in Munster — I did not like it there one bit! The people of the town have always had a reputation for not liking us and it certainly showed. I believe it is still the same now; the troops are just not welcome there.

I had another problem to contend with now, however. I was the only regular private soldier in the entire camp. This was apparently because the Government had changed the policy on National Service men in the last months of their service. If they were in BAOR they would serve two and a half years, an extra six months, while those at home finished after two years, and many of those in the UK who had only a short time to go, were sent to Germany for six months. So being a regular soldier I was not popular at all.

Here, I came in for a fair spot of bullying. It was never physical, but I was made to feel a complete outsider and it was not an enjoyable time for me at all, although I did qualify as a Class One driver, which enabled me to enjoy myself driving big trucks. This had been my intention all along and at least made life somewhat more bearable.

But even this "treat" was a limited one. The unit was a stores one attached to REME workshops and most of the vehicles were left stationary most of the time, loaded with stores that would be needed if we went to war — all ready to go out into the field.

Efficient organisation it might have been, keeping us at a constant state of readiness, but it meant that all the keen young drivers on the base had to take turns making the runs that came up, so to add a spot of interest to my life I managed to get into the recovery side, spending quite a bit of time with REME's recovery crews. I got on extremely well with them and spent a good deal of time driving huge Scammel trucks. Great fun!

Overall however, when I weighed things up, I was still not happy. Germany was turning out to be a mistake and so I began to save my wages to buy myself out. To be allowed to do this you had to have served for three years and it cost £350. It was a good deal of money, but it seemed, at the time, well worth it.

Then, while I was ticking off the days, weeks and months towards the three years, I was posted again. This time it was back to England, to the Army Methods of Instruction Centre at Warminster.

Now, I had become a batman, driving a staff car or mini bus, with the task of looking after the needs of two majors. Suddenly, this was to my liking! I had a good deal of time off and considerable independence.

One of the officers for whom I worked, Major Guy MC of the Queen's Surrey Regiment, and his wife, were exceptionally kind to me. It was thoroughly enjoyable working for them and to this day I call and see them whenever I am in their home town.

By this time I had been promoted to lance corporal and my single stripe brought with it the magnificent sum of seven and sixpence a day extra pay. Now, I was given the responsibility of ensuring that the accommodation for the senior NCOs arriving for the course, was ready for them. I had about twenty rooms to oversee and had to make sure that all their bedding and other requirements were in order.

And it was here that my early experience in the catering trade came racing to my aid.

The accommodation block was not part of the sergeants' mess complex and I was able to offer the NCOs my own mess service — tea or coffee in the morning with their early calls, with a newspaper if required.

Soon, I had this organised with clockwork precision, bringing in my own supply of tea, coffee and sugar, with my own delivery of milk arriving each morning. This was all perfectly above board. My superiors knew all about it and it certainly added a most welcome sum to my income, for, almost without exception, every man took me up on my offer at sixpence per day. I also added in the service of making the beds and received handsome tips at the end of the courses, ten bob being quite a common reward for my efforts.

This was a job that was enabling me to put my catering skills to good use in more than one direction, for in the evenings my time was my own and I soon obtained a job as a part-time barman at the Bath Arms in Warminster where I worked for quite some time.

The money was now coming in quite nicely thanks to my little spot of private enterprise. Soon, I would have enough to buy that one way ticket back to civvy street .... and yet, I was doing so well now that a little voice began to tell me that perhaps the Army was not such a bad place after all .... and after a while another idea came to me.

Instead of putting my fund to buying my discharge, I decided to spend it on a new car. So, in 1964, the cash I had so carefully saved and slaved for, I added to a spot of hire purchase — and blew the lot on a new car!

It was a Mini, one of the first to have the new hydrolastic suspension and it cost me £515 18s. 2d. exactly. "Worth every penny" I congratulated myself as I looked at AWV 904B. It was brand new, with gleaming blue paintwork — and it was all mine! My first new car. My pride and joy. I could not have been prouder.

To my intense chagrin it did not stay in line with the maker's specifications for long when I proudly drove it home the week-end after I had bought it.

Valerie and I were still courting. We had kept in touch when I first went to Germany and of course, once I returned to the UK saw more of each other. While I was still working for my father I worked week-ends and some evenings at the club and I quickly realised that if I was to have a chance of hanging on to the "Vision" I had to occupy her while I was working — so I got her to help out behind the bar and after I joined the Army she had continued to work for my parents.

Now I had my own transport again it became even easier to get home to see her and we decided to christen the Mini by taking her parents to Blackpool to see the illuminations. But on the way back to Bramhall, in the queues that inevitably form on the roads leading out of the town as visitors make their way home after "seeing the lights", we had a lucky escape.

We were stopped at traffic lights with a coach on our offside. As the lights changed I moved forward. The coach driver did not, wise man! Unknown to me he had seen a Jaguar jumping the lights from the right. I had not seen this idiot and carried on and the next thing I knew, the Jag had hit us on the front offside, and spun us round in the road. We were all shaken up, but not hurt and my next thought was to give the clown in the other car a hard time. But as I climbed out I could see his tail lights disappearing fast as he roared away into the night.

29

All I could say in disbelief was: "He's not stopping! He's not stopping!"

The car was quite severely damaged at the front and it took some time for us to move it as the wing had been bashed in on to the wheel and we could not steer it. There was a garage nearby, however and they got us running again.

I was surprised that the only vehicle to stop was a car load of Asian lads who happened to be going our way home and who followed us all the way back to Manchester to make sure we made it without further mishap. It was a very touching inter-racial gesture which was greatly appreciated.

One week's ownership. One crash. What a sickener! But at least the car was adequately insured and within ten days it was back on the road.

I was also now "back on the road" as far as my Army career was concerned. I had become quite happy with the way things were. The only snag was the fact that promotion looked a long way away. Being an RAOC driver was to wait for dead men's shoes I had discovered; there were a great many people ahead of me in the promotion stakes. If they were not better qualified they certainly had more experience, so it was obvious where any stripes that were handed out would go.

But this was where I had another stroke of good fortune in meeting up with Warrant Officer Cant, who was in charge of the ammunition side of the main unit at the School of Infantry's main barracks at Warminster.

During a long natter to him I mentioned my fears about the lack of advancement that was likely to be open to me and he said:

"Well, why don't you become an ammunition technician?"

"What's that?" I asked.

"You deal with ammunition" he said "You go on a course — and then it's full corporal straight away",

"That's for me!" I replied "How do I apply?"

"I'll do the necessary and get you an inteview" he promised.

Sure enough, he was as good as his word and within a very short time I was called to the Ammunition Inspectorate, Southern Command at Wilton to meet the Senior Ammunition Technical Officer.

We went through the usual interview routine until he asked: "Why do you want to do this?"

"Well, I like taking things apart" I explained brightly "I like fiddling with things".

"Ammunition technicians do not fiddle. They know exactly what they are doing!" he bridled, putting me firmly in my place with egg all over my face.

I left cursing my big mouth and thought: "Oh well. That's that". But to my surprise, several weeks later, I received an order, saying that I had been selected for the 1966 AT's course and was to report to the Central Ammunition Depot, Bramley on a set date.

So began my association with the ammunition world as I duly reported for the course along with about sixteen other hopefuls. It was a twelve-month course, which only twelve of us were to complete successfully, and it covered all aspects of Army ammo, including guided missiles, with the second stripe and the coveted "A"-in-flame trade badge the reward for those who passed out.

The course was a tough one, but half way through it I had a pleasant diversion from it when Valerie and I were married! I was the proudest soldier in the British Army that day as I kept my most important date with my "Vision", putting on my best turnout in my No. 1 dress uniform and supported by two Army mates, Geordie Collins, my best man, and Bill Sutton.

Val and I were not entitled to married quarters at that stage, but found a "hiring", accommodation which we had to provide for ourselves and to which the Ministry of Defence paid part of the rent so that we paid the same rate as for military accommodation.

It suited us well enough, but as for married bliss, well, Mrs Callaghan had to wait a while for that, because I still had the serious business of the course to pass and while I applied myself to that she was virtually a grass widow.

The course was so rigorous that a pass mark of 65 per cent was required for each section and if you failed one major exam, you packed your books and off you went. Consequently, I and two lads with whom I had palled up, Merv Chapman and Steve Emerson, got together at our house to burn the midnight oil in a determined bid to ensure that we did not blow our big chance.

The senior ATO I had seen at Wilton was dead right when he had said that ammunition technicians knew exactly what they were doing!

But at long last, all our hard graft was rewarded. We all passed and I was pleased to find that I had finished equal third.

The last I heard, Merv was a captain and Steve had reached major, so both had put their hard-gleaned knowledge to good use.

Now a qualified AT, with my two stripes and my "A"-in-flame on my sleeve, I was posted to the Central Ammunition Depot at Kineton. Valerie now began to get a taste of what it is like to be an Army wife, constantly on the move, as we had to move again. Because the Army would not take on any more hirings at that time we had to rent private accommodation. We took a flat in an old house of some considerable standing where, we were quite amused to hear, it was said that Nell Gwynne had entertained the members of the aristocracy in her heyday!

We lived there for twelve months, until we heard of a little cottage that was for rent in the small village of Avon Dassett. This was owned by a retired Colonel Worrall, whose wife ran the housing side of one of Warwickshire's large manor farms, hiring out several of their properties to the Army.

Colonel and Mrs. Worrall had a daughter who married a Welsh Guards Officer, who rose to become Commanding Officer of his battalion. By chance, years later, I had the privilege of supporting him when based at Bessbrook, though it took a chat at dinner to which I had been invited, one night, in the officers' mess, when I was seated next to the Colonel, for us to discover the connection and just what a small world it is.

I had always been kidded, during my service life, about my size, naturally enough, typically Army humour branding me as "short arse" and making me the butt of various jokes.

There was one aspect of being short that worked to my advantage however, in that , whenever there was a parade the rule was always tallest to the right, shortest to the left, and while the others were always fumbling about and eyeing each other as to whether they were slightly taller or shorter than the next bloke I didn't have that sort of problem and made the outside left position my own!

During the three years I spent at Kineton the leg pulling went on, but it was here that a new word was unofficially introduced to Army technology. Now, the holes we produced on the demolition ground were no longer measured in feet and inches, but in "Callaghans" instead, so that a hole say, four feet deep would be solemnly referred to as being one and a half Callaghans in depth. Fame at last! It was a term that stuck and was all in good fun.

While I was stationed at Kineton a number of us were sent back to Bramley on an upgrading course. This marked the next step in my advancement; it was an intensive training course which had to be undertaken before any more promotion would come my way. Here I learned considerably more about ammunition and making things go bang. It was my first encounter with old and dangerous ammo and blowing things up outside an authorised demolition area.

The end of the course marked a new posting that I knew I was due and I was delighted to learn that I was being sent to the one ammunition inspection and disposal unit, which was the forerunner of 11 EOD Regiment RLC, as it is now. I was posted to Barlow in Yorkshire not far from Selby and considered myself a lucky lad as some of my colleagues went off from one central ammuniton depot to another.

I spent a year in Yorkshire, which is an agreeable part of the world to live, and put the time to good use, steadily building up my expertise and learning a great deal more about explosions in confined areas.

Now, Valerie and I had our married quarters. Our son, David, was born at York on February 17th 1971, and all was well with my world. I had come a long way from being an outcast, short-sighted, short-arsed kid on the streets of Ancoats and felt my star was definitely in the ascendancy.

Life in the Army can throw up a good many surprises and I was handed one when it was announced that I was to go on an unaccompanied tour of Bahrain to do depot-type work. So, while Valerie went back to her mother's in Bramhall, I headed off to the sunshine!

My lack of size has given me some hassle over the years, there's no denying that, but while I was in Bahrain it proved an asset in an unusual and novel way. Because of my lack of inches I was selected to do some work for the local Sheikh, who had his own bodyguard company. It appeared that his stock of ammunition was causing him some concern and we had been approached to see if we would help. I was selected as the man for the job — purely because I was small! This surprising qualification that suddenly leaped out of the Army regulations came about because, I was told, I was the only man in the unit who would not look down on the Sheikh, who was only 5ft 3ins. The major who selected me for the task, Tom Judge, was tall and he came along to smooth the way in the public relations role, but it appeared that it mattered not what size an officer was, but to have a corporal look down on the local desert leader just would not do so far as protocol was concerned.

It was the strangest qualification for a job I had ever come across and I was told, in no uncertain terms, that it was also hush-hush and I was not to breathe a word to anybody. This was because the Sheikh was not strictly allowed to have a private army and we had to go off in civilian clothes, being collected by an air-conditioned Mercedes which whisked us off into the desert like a couple of spies!

We were taken to a building which had two distinct and very differing functions. Not only was it the armoury, but also, I discovered later, the harem! There was not a wife, or concubine in sight, but the treasures in the place staggered me. In a room big enough, I calculated, to comfortably hold at least three snooker tables, was a collection of treasures that made me think I had wandered into Aladdin's cave. The floor was covered with so many Persian carpets — there must have been at least eight layers — that you had to step up into the room, but it was the sight that greeted me as I stepped in that took my breath away.

In the centre of the room were several huge dining tables piled high with all manner of valuables .... beautiful model silver dhows, oil paintings, silver trophies, porcelain, china, silver tableware. It was a fortune by any standards.

But he went in for a bizarre mixture of items did our Sheikh, because all around the walls of the room were gun racks, totally incongruous among such exquisite wealth and beauty. There were rifles, pistols, light and heavy machine guns — none of which was secured.

A senior cousin of the Sheikh had been detailed to meet us and show us our task — after the usual niceties of tea had been observed, of course.

Just off the Aladdin's cave was a room in which a guard had been assigned to act as my assistant while I went to work on the ammunition. There were thousands of rounds of varying calibres, as well as grenades, all piled in the room, and certainly not stacked, as our regulations required it to be. This treatment of ammunition would not have been allowed under our rules, so I set to work to sort it out.

Some time earlier, the Sheikh had armed his body-guards with the ammo — whether for an exercise or in earnest I knew not — but when they had returned it they had simply dumped it in a wooden chest and now it was in very poor condition. The fact that it had been handled, with the grease from human hands getting on to it and had been left outside for a spell in that climate, had caused it to deteriorate.

While I was working on the bullets, the major was cataloguing the weapons, with the aid of the guard, though the guard had no idea he was helping in this way at the time! I had made a gesture, earlier, to see one of the weapons from the racks and the guard had been keen to show his skills, so that when I cocked a machine gun to check whether it was empty in the normal safety procedure and found I did not know how to let the working parts go forward again, our man eagerly showed me how it operated. He needed no encouraging to show the Major how all the other weapons worked. Thank you very much! We were thus able to assess exactly what was stored there and in this way a covert operation was quickly carried out under the nose of the guard.

During lunch on the second day, the Sheikh himself came to check on our progress and was highly pleased when I briefed him, eye to eye so to speak, on what measures he should take to bring his stock of ammo up to scratch.

I had never come across anybody before who was reputed to have six million dollars a year personal expenses — and he was one of the poor relations among the sheikhs!

I was warmly thanked by the Sheikh through his interpreter and via his own broken English and was handed a small white box which he produced from a shabby pvc bag which looked for all the world as though it could contain the vegetables for dinner. To my surprise, the box contained a gold Tissot wristwatch which was, it seemed, a customary gift. I was not allowed to relate this story to my mates back at camp. My lips had to remain sealed and while the watch is now somewhat dated, it still keeps pretty good time.

My time in the Middle East ended with a trip to Sharjah in the United Arab Emirates, where I became local acting sergeant to oversee the shipment of all the UK explosives from there due to the closure of our depot.

I had made sergeant at last — but it did not last long. On returning to the UK I was posted to the central ammunition depot at Longtown in Cumbria. It was back to corporal again, but it was not bad because the corporals were the lowest rank there and were equal members of the sergeant's mess. The workforce was mainly civilian and I was not to know it then, but I was to be extremely glad of that fact many years later when I got a job there on leaving the Army.

We were back together as a family again when Valerie and David joined me with a married quarter readily available in Carlisle, though other moves were afoot that would provide me with the toughest test of my career.

The unrest in Northern Ireland was big media news now. The RAOC sergeants were heavily involved in operations over there and we corporals saw this as a chance to do a "real job" and looked forward to going too.

We all wanted to get "over the water" before the troubles finished. Who could have known that most of us would go twice in the next eighteen to twenty years?

CHAPTER 4

St Peter's Page

MY class at the Army School of Ammunition were assembling ready to listen to my lecture on methods of entering suspect vehicles when I received a piece of news that shook me to the core.

Vernon Rose had been killed in Northern Ireland while tackling a car bomb.

Vernon had been one of my pupils at the school, where I was now a sergeant instructor, and I now had to go into the lecture room and give a presentation to the course, just minutes after hearing of his death. I was in a daze, but in the Army, as on the stage, the show has to go on, but though I got through the lecture I did it totally on auto pilot and had no recollection afterwards of what I had said. At the end of the class I announced that we had just heard that Vernon had been killed by a booby trap and it was a very sombre group of candidates who left the room. It had brought it home to them.

It got home to me too. I knew Vernon extremely well and the thought that kept going round in my mind was: Had I not told him something? Had I failed to give him a tip that could have saved him? All tips that were collected were passed among us, but of course you cannot tell everybody everything, although that fact did not help me as I wrestled with the question: Had I failed him?

Later, we learned that the device had been a good

"come on" and could have trapped anybody so, unhappily, it was simply his turn to go.

In situations such as this I have always been helped by my fatalistic outlook and my belief that we all die at an appointed time.

Whenever you read about a major disaster — an air crash, say, it is a certainty that next day the newspapers will carry follow-up stories of a "lucky" person or family who, for some reason, missed the flight. Or, sadly, there will be one about the passenger who was switched to that particular aircraft unexpectedly.

There is inevitably speculation about such incidents: how the person who escaped was in God's hands or had a guardian angel and the fact that somebody perished who "should not have done" was sheer bad luck.

No doubt the loved ones of such victims say to themselves: "If only he hadn't caught that plane he'd be alive today", while the one who escapes will, if he is religious, give thanks that he was spared.

Yet, to my mind, in the normal run of things in the twists and turns of life, if you are due to die in any circumstances there is NOTHING you can do about it. As they say in the well-worn phrase: If your name is on the bullet you are dead.

I am a firm believer in this: a fatalist. To me, wherever you are and whatever you are doing, if St Peter turns that day to a page with your name on it and he says "Callaghan, it's you next" you go. It's your time. To me it is as simple as that.

Of course, I'm not stupid enough to believe that if it's not my time I can go out and behave like a lunatic and bear a charmed life in which no harm will befall me; I know full well that if I go out and stand in the middle of the M1 then something is going to come along and despatch me to my maker without further ado. But in your normal sphere of life, when you have got to go you've got to go — and not before.

How does this affect a soldier, who may fairly be said to put himself in more dangerous situations than the average civilian? And does not the fact that at some time he will almost certainly be serving in Northern Ireland mean that he will stand a greater chance of St Peter turning to the page with his name on it?

Not in my view it doesn't. To a soldier, this is his normal way of life anyway. He is doing what he has chosen to do in being a member of the armed forces, so he is not adding any extra element of danger to his life. It is what he does.

As for Northern Ireland, it always seems terrible to the folks back home when they read of some dreadful incident, and so it is. But in fact, statistically, a soldier is far safer facing the possible threat of terrorist action there than in his normal life elsewhere, for more soldiers are killed in road accidents each year than die in the Province. In fact, N.I. can be a mindlessly boring place and when troops there read in the papers of all the murders, rapes and muggings going on at home it can seem quiet by comparison.

In my own field, though bomb disposal experts are often talked about as being terribly brave in facing up to lurking objects that may blow them to pieces at any second, they are no braver than anybody else. In fact, there is no way I could go out on patrol in the way that the infantry do, waiting to be shot at, or blown up by a hidden bomb.

When the bomb disposal operator—or 'Felix'—goes out on a job, at least he can see more or less what he is up against, and I always believed that the standard of my training and the quality of our equipment should see me through in normal circumstances, provided I approached the job in the correct manner.

But there will always be tragedies however careful we are and my beliefs did not make these any easier to take.

My earliest experience of a tragedy in which the circumstances were definitely "unfair" concerned my cousin Christine. She was aged nine when she was killed by the most dreadful piece of "bad luck" imaginable.

Christine was a monitor at her school in Rochdale where one of her duties was to take the teacher her tea at playtime, after which she went off to join the rest of the kids on their break. Work was being done on the roof of the school and as she went through the door into the playground one of the coping stones from the roof chose that time to fall. It crushed her so badly that she was identifiable only by the clothing she was wearing.

Nine years old, going through a door that had apparently not been tied, or locked in any way, though the area outside was cordoned off. The only child involved, leaving the building as a stone hurtled down at precisely the wrong time. What on earth had the poor girl done to deserve such a fate?

The things I can remember being said at the time that had a profound effect on me was that Heaven is not made up of old and sick people and that children are only loaned to us and that God can take them back at any time.

That may be so. But I'm sure that it was that statement that put Christine's father, my Uncle Harold, off completely. It was a harsh thing to be said at the time when you have lost your only child and from that day Uncle has not been in a church except for my father's funeral in 1982 after I had returned from the Falklands.

But it is true that God moves in mysterious ways, because a couple of years after the tragedy Harold and Aunt

Ally went in for fostering children. Now, at the age of more than 70, Harold and his wife have brought comfort and a good home to hundreds of kids who would otherwise have suffered. So out of the death of poor hapless Christine so many others have benefited.

I have heard of the deaths of numerous colleagues over the years, unhappily, though I found that these affected me in differing ways.

In the early days of the Northern Ireland situation I was called over there because Major Bernard Calladine and Sergeant Chris Cracknell had been killed by a car bomb. I had met the major but knew him only as a senior officer. Chris I had not met. There is a chill that runs through you when you hear of fellow soldiers being killed, but in the case of these two poor fellows I felt distant from the tragedy because I did not know them personally.

When I lost another colleague I had to go to Lurgan the next day to do one of "his" jobs, which gave me a sick feeling. Again, though sad, I felt distant from the tragedy, but it was vastly different for his mates in the Omagh detachment. He had been killed picking up the bits of mortars after an attack. While he was collecting one of them it went off for some reason and I found the lads with whom he worked devastated by their loss as had been those who worked with the two killed by the car bomb. They were all in a state of shock and clearly felt their loss as I had felt that of Vernon Rose.

My philosophy that, whatever I chose to do in life, if it was my turn to go I would go and there was nothing I could do about it, has always helped me in my job. this applies particularly to Northern Ireland, a world of booby traps and totally ruthless people among those who have decided to wage a terrorist war against us. But there was one thing I had made my mind up about when I first realised I was going over there, and that was, that if fate allowed, if I was going to make a mistake I was going to make it a good one.

No way did I want to survive an incident as a cabbage. If something went wrong I did not want to be so severely injured that I would be a burden on my family or to whoever would fall the task of looking after me. To be left with all my other faculties, but permanently paralysed, seeing what was going on around me, was not for me. So if I got it wrong I hoped I would do so in a conclusive way and go out with a bloody big bang so that I did not hear it — and they could pick me up from all over Fermanagh, Tyrone, Armagh or wherever.

Fortunately, I did not make that sort of mistake, though there were times when it was desperately close, when I thought "Phew! You got away with that one, Kevin," but in normal civilian life I'm sure most people have noticed these sort of near misses. You can be driving along a country lane, for instance, in the early hours of the morning and as you come to a crossroads, sure enough, another vehicle will flash across coming the other way at that precise moment, so that had you crossed it would have hit you. Yet, you could sit there for ages waiting for another car and not see one for hours.

Why do such things happen? Why does a tree choose a precise moment to fall as a car is passing and kill the driver? Why should cousin Christine be taken so cruelly, so young, as the "reward" for doing a good turn for somebody? And why should Vernon Rose, one of the nicest people you could wish to meet, have to die?

There are countless examples such as these and I'm sure we can all quote a few that have struck home to us on a personal level and caused immense distress while leaving us wondering why so many wicked people remain unscathed.

It's clear to me that people in "dangerous" jobs develop

a similar attitude to my own. In his autobiography, the great test pilot, Chuck Yeager, says: "After umpteen hours of research flying I became a fatalist. I was damned aware of the dangers, but I didn't dwell on them or let them spook me. Taking risks was my job, and if I were destined to be blown to pieces on the next flight, there probably wasn't a whole helluva lot I could do to prevent it from happening."

There is obviously some system for choosing who goes and when, but for the life of me I can't fathom what it is. It's a most unfair system. It really is.

CHAPTER 5

First Blood

DISCO? Surely my ears were deceiving me! Yet, I could have sworn that was what I had just heard being announced as the highlight of the evening's entertainment.

As I listened with ill-concealed horror I realised that, unfortunately, my ears were in perfect working order and the group of soldiers with whom I was to spend the next few hours, had indeed, laid on a knees-up.

Now, under normal circumstances, that would have been fine by me. I like a good time as much as the next bloke, but this was Northern Ireland in 1972 and I had just arrived to play my part in Her Majesty's Forces' struggle against terrorism.

I had been scared for the greater part of the few days I had been there, convinced I was going to be shot or blown to bits every time I went out in public .... and yet here were a bunch of lunatics planning a disco. And what really staggered me about their little scheme was that they had invited the local female talent into the barracks to take part!

The situation was becoming more bizarre by the minute. The "do" was being held in the quaintly named "Virg Inn" in the barracks at Lurgan, which turned out to be an old knicker factory. Headlines flashed through my mind that would probably be read in tomorrow morning's papers as Callaghan's brave career in the Province ended before it had started: "Knees up in the knicker factory" was swiftly replaced by "Knicker factory massacre" or, in the local Press perhaps, "Knickers to the British Army!"

It just didn't bear thinking about. I had made it all the way from England, through the terrors of the car journey, safely into the sanctuary of the barracks and here were locals being invited inside. What sort of security was this?

"Have they all been checked?" I asked, trying, but failing, I suspected, to hide my concern.

"Oh yes, they've all been checked out." I was assured. There was nothing for it, but to sit back and hope they had done their checking thoroughly.

The entertainment was being held on the territory of 321 Section EOD Company who had been in the building longer than any other company and are certainly one of, if not the, longest-serving unit in Northern Ireland. While others came and went, they stayed and they had things beautifully organised, with a rest room and a dance area, complete with their Virg-Inn. What a set-up!

I was being sucked, unwillingly, into this situation by virtue of the fact that I had to sit tight and wait for my team to arrive from Omagh, to where I was to be whisked off in a move that, in itself, had come as a shock to me shortly after I had arrived.

The Omagh lads were due down that night to collect some equipment and when they duly arrived I was keen to get to know everything that was going on — only to find the confounded lot of them had eyes only for the disco.

This was serious and there was only one thing to do so—I joined in the dancing with the rest of them!

Come ten o'clock however, and the nod went round for the team to leave for Omagh. I was not too bothered about the journey there as it was dark and the record of attacks on vehicles during the hours of darkness were very low.

What a contrast this was to my mental state a few hours earlier, on the journey down to Lurgan from Lisburn.

I had been given my first taste of life "over the water" with a two-day induction course in Lisburn, during which I had been told generally what was going on in an up-to-date briefing, during which I had fired the nine-millimetre Browning, the regulation issue side-arm.

As part of the course there was a visit to Ballykinler ammunition depot, on which I learned the hard way of the scariness of travelling by road over there. Even though we were travelling in an unmarked "Q" car, I fully expected to be blown up every time we passed over a culvert, or shot every time the vehicle had to halt in traffic or at a road junction.

Lisburn, as it happened, was considered to be a "safe" place in those days, but I was still convinced I was going to get mortared in my sleep.

I was convinced everybody was looking at me in recognition; the nine-millimetre Browning, with its 13 rounds, was burning a hole in my back, where it nestled in my trouser waistband and I knew that I looked like the Hunchback of Notre Dame with it stuck there.

It was during the course that I learned I would be going to where the Brigade was based in the knicker factory just outside the town centre. I was driven down there in a "Q" car, still convinced every yard of the way, that I was about to be zapped. It was terrible. But as we entered the town after an uneventful drive down the motorway, I was surprised to see people doing normal things. They were actually shopping, they were waiting for buses—and the shops were still standing. It came as a complete shock that there were no signs of bombing at all when I suppose

I had been expecting sights similar to the effects of the blitz during the war.

We were almost there, but there was another moment of tension for me as we turned off the main street and into the factory gates where our identities were checked. I was petrified! It was obvious to a blind man that only security forces vehicles would drive into the barracks and even though we were in an unmarked car I expected to be gunned down at any second.

After what seemed ages the gates opened to allow us in and I breathed a sigh of relief. Made it! That was my first big assignment over—and that was just getting there.

But there was another shock in store for me. I began to feel a little better when I spotted the familiar Landrovers and horse box-type trailer of the EOD company, but I'd no sooner entered the office than I was greeted with: "Welcome. We were wondering where you were. Get yourself some tea, because you're off to Omagh."

Panic! I'd only just begun to relax after my spot of Russian roulette with the terrorists on the way there, and they were sending me out as a target again. Not only that, I'd given Val the Lurgan address — and now I was not going to be there.

"How long for?" I asked "Oh, at least until R and R" I was told. That was normally about two and a half months into the tour when you got three or four day's rest and recuperation.

I did not like the sound of this at all. The problem with Omagh, as I saw it was that it was regarded as a quiet place, with very little EOD work and the tactical area of responsibility was quite large, covering the whole of Fermanagh and Tyrone. It was a long way from Lurgan and you were on your own, with just your team, and were tasked by the resident battalion.

This worried me, for at the time they were the 16th/5th

Queen's Royal Lancers. The cavalry are a "different" lot, no doubt about it. Would they understand our specific needs? I wondered, or would they treat me just like a disposable asset. I could not think of one advantage of going to Omagh.

But there was nothing I could do about it, so I went off for my tea — a plate of beef stroganoff and rice, which lifted my spirits a little, while my vastly more experienced colleagues, some with as much as two months' service there, related their war stories. I had no idea who they were talking about as they told how "so-and-so" had been picked up and how "thingy" was being watched. This was their up-to-the-minute report on the state of the game with the local "players", and I did my best to look as though I understood what was what and managed to slip in the odd question about kit etc.

"You'll get the hang of it" they nonchalantly reassured me.

The captain who was the ATO in charge, had returned from a task by the time I'd finished my meal and briefed me on my new location. He made it sound reasonable enough — but I would certainly have felt a whole lot better if I had known, as I found out later, that they put only their most competent operators, those who had done particularly well on their courses, out in the outlying areas, where they could be relied upon to work without supervision.

I wasn't the Army's happiest fella as the disco ended— for us anyway—and we loaded up the Landrovers for the trip to Omagh, but orders were orders, so I just had to get on with it.

Attacks on vehicles at night may have been infrequent, but I still kept my eyes peeled, trying to look for landmarks to familiarise myself with the area. I did not drink alcohol at that time, but I was high on adrenalin once more, conscious of the fact that our convoy of two vehicles obviously belonged to the Army as it wound its way along the roads, though the darkness was a comforting cloak.

But I relaxed again as we arrived safely at the camp and as we began unloading I noticed my No. 2 did not disarm a Browning 9mm pistol as the rest of us did, but produced instead a Browning shotgun. This was loaded with five cartridges, with nine balls per cartridge, and it was explained to me that a shotgun had far greater firepower at close range than a sub machine gun on automatic. A very anti-social weapon indeed and I felt a good deal better knowing that was what we had been carrying for our own close personal protection.

I found myself billeted in a transit room for the time being, because the ATOs room was still occupied by the operator from whom I was to take over when he left in a few days time.

Throughout the following day, having met the various personnel of the 16th/5th and the helicopter lads from the Army Air Corps, I waited to be called out to tackle my first job. But the call did not come. Nor was I called on the second day. I began to fret about the situation. Normally, during my settling in period, the system would be for me to go out on call with the senior operator to see how to operate in that particular area during a couple of tasks and then I would do one myself under his guidance and if I came through my "trial" I would go it alone when he left. But two days had passed without a chance to go through this procedure, and the senior man was going home in two days. The third day passed—and still no job. I spent the time getting to know the area and the Security Forces out-stations at places such as Enniskillen and Belleek, but at least this served one useful purpose as I found the anxiety of driving around the country roads

51

lessened every time we went out. I realised that if you did not move at a regular time and use a regular route the chances of getting zapped were quite small. Anyway, I travelled in the lead vehicle and it was a comfort to remind myself that it was the second or third one that invariably copped it from a mine or bomb. If you were still killed having taken every possible precaution, then there was very little you could do about it anyway.

As fate would have it, the day for my senior to leave arrived and I still hadn't been out on a job, so he just wished me luck and left me to it! I watched him leaving by "Q" car for Lurgan, knowing that he would be having a party there that night before flying home the next day and thought: "God. I wish it was me."

Now I really was in at the deep end on my own. But I set to work making things more to my liking and, like all new brooms, changed things around—probably back to where they had been before my predecessor arrived. Then, I went off and sat in the ATOs room in the mess and felt very alone.

My No. 2, who also acted as my driver, had been there for a whole three months, so I knew I had some experience I could count on, and our escort, a team of four from the Lancers, were old hands—but I still felt alone.

During the last four days I had realised that apart from the carrying of loaded weapons and the armoured Ferret scout cars running around all the time, life in Omagh was quite normal. Soldiers even went out in pairs to certain pubs and hotels.

As for life inside the barracks, the food on the sergeants' mess was absolutely first class. This was my first experiene of a cavalry unit's way of life and I learned that they do things very differently from other regiments. In the cavalry, for instance, the RSM did not just think he was God. He knew he was!

I was made to feel very welcome by this somewhat unusual group and my feeling of being alone gradually vanished as I settled into the environment.

I was still untried, wondering when my first solo job would come up, when the phone rang in mid-morning with a request for the ATO to go to the ops room. My heart missed a beat. What had I done? Or what hadn't I done? Or could it even be a task for me at long last?

Shouting to my team to stand by I went across the road to the Headquarters building where the duty watchkeeper informed me that a milk churn had been found on the road leading to Gortin Ranges — military rifle ranges which were still in use. A council workman, with a hedge-cutting tractor, had uncovered the churn and had seen a white wire coming out of the lid.

My mind began to work overtime as I quickly identified it as a possible claymore device. This is a milk churn which is half-filled with nuts and bolts, nails and various bits of scrap metal — dockyard confetti in bomb disposal parlance — the rest of the churn is filled with explosive and pointed at the target.

When this little lot goes off, normally being initiated via a command wire of considerable length leading to a vantage point where it is attached to a battery and a bell push, it does so with a gigantic blunderbuss effect which will make a mess of a car or any soft-skinned military vehicle.

"At last! This is it!" I thought as my pulse began to quicken. "Think, think. Go through the steps you have been taught. Ask the right questions."

But after I had established the exact location of the device and whether any of our patrols were in the area, I left the ops room in a daze to brief the team, still urging myself "Think! think!" as I tried to gather my wits on the short walk back to where the team were waiting for me to lead them off.

"What is it? Where is it?" The team asked eagerly, as I got back. They were straining at the leash to go, with their flak jackets on already.

As I recounted the brief details one of the escorts casually mentioned that there had been a booby trap on the ranges some months earlier. I stopped in full flow.

"What? Tell me about it!" I ordered.

He said that a firing point had been booby-trapped, so I looked through the file and sure enough a clever, yet simple pressure switch had been placed in the ground where a soldier would lie when firing in the prone position. But a further check revealed that it was the only other incident in the area, so armed with this information, we set off with a Ferret leading the way as escort.

The significance of this was not lost on me. "God! I'm in the second vehicle" I realised with a feeling of dread as the adrenalin pumped around my body at full whack. I went over and over the various points of information as we drove the eight miles to the area. Suddenly the vehicle slowed and I looked up in surprise to see a road block.

For a second I panicked, only to realise it was our road block. We were there already at the incident control point and as I got out I found the section leader and the council worker waiting for me.

"Here goes" I thought as I walked to meet them on my first job. At least I had a nice day for it—a sunny crisp October morning. Now it was down to me to show what I could do.

The tractor driver said he had been cutting the hedge when his cutter had struck what he took to be a stone, but on going to clear it he found a creamery can, as they called them locally, with a wire coming from the lid.

I asked him to show me and we walked together for a

close-up to where a tangle of gorse, bramble and bracken were waiting to be cut. At the bottom of the ditch could be seen the object of his concern, a rusty churn, with its tell-tale wire.

The obvious course was to put a small charge on it and destroy it in situ, so I set to work preparing a small amount of plastic explosive with a primer, known as a PE bomb.

Clad in my bomb suit I set off on the notorious Lonely Walk to the device while I asked myself whether I had forgotten anything. I placed the explosive on the neck of the churn and taped it in place, fully mindful of the fact that the contents of the churn would vapourise me if it went off now. My suit would not protect me against something that big at close quarters.

But I realised it was just like being in training only without the instructor peering over my shoulder and the training took over automatically: get in, carry out the plan and get out, was the drill, spending as little time at the device as possible.

I went back to the control point feeling quite relieved. So far so good. Word of the impending bang was passed around, then, after I had shouted the customary warning: "boom!" a cloud of dirt and shrubbery went skywards, scattering bits of hedge all over the road.

The section commander and I went to take a look at the hole, which was some three metres across and a metre deep. I stood admiring my handiwork, thinking that it was far quicker than cutting hedges by tractor, when the sergeant said:

"Hey Kevin. You've seen that one over there, haven't you?" pointing to another churn which had been partly exposed by the blast.

"No. I haven't" I said and we started running back to the control point as fast as we could.

"We've found another one!" I told the bomb crew.

"Jesus!" said the tractor driver.

Back to Square One. This time, I decided to rely on one of our old stand-bys and hook and line the churn into the space created by the explosion, using a heavy duty tow rope and a telegraph pole as a fulcrum as the undergrowth around the can was pretty thick.

This would make it easy to dispose of and would limit damage to the hedge. Simple, but effective. Or so I thought.

So off I went again. I was now reasonably in control of my fear as I had been to the area twice and was still alive. Alas, this state of mind did not last long.

I scrambled down the bank to get the rope around the telegraph pole and as I clambered in among the gorse and brambles to squeeze past the pole one foot slipped and I fell about eighteen inches—or what turned out to be the width of a milk churn, for as I looked down I froze in my tracks. For there between my legs was another churn! I had been standing on the damned thing when I had lost my footing and now there it was ready to do God knows what to me if it went off.

I began to panic, then quickly got a grip of myself. Why panic? I was still in one piece, the situation had not changed and there was a job to be done—so I made myself get on with it as calmly as I could.

I attached the rope to the handle of the second churn, then fed it through the handle of the third. Two for the price of one, I thought.

When I returned to the ICP and told the team the news they whistled through their teeth in grim surprise. The situation was not lost on the tractor driver either.

"Jee-sus!" he said.

The Landrover was used to pull the rope, which

stretched mightily, until suddenly the churn catapulted out of the brambles. So far, so good.

I left it for a few minutes while I prepared two more PE bombs, then, for the fourth time, I cautiously approached again. This time it was a sight for sore eyes. The two churns, neatly roped together, lay side by side in the spot I wanted. As I released the rope one of them moved slightly, giving me a nasty moment, but I got the tackle clear without further problem, placed the charges and went back again to warn of an even bigger bang.

"Stand by. Firing" Then—boom!

"Jeee-sus!" I heard from behind me as smoke billowed upwards and bits of churn, telegraph pole, earth, gorse and brambles showered down around us.

"Mmm. Could have moved back a bit" I thought rue-fully, but fortunately, nobody was hurt and that, I hoped, was that.

Back I went yet again and this time made a careful in-spection of the area to make sure there were no more hid-den presents lurking in the undergrowth. Then, it was time to clear up and I allowed everybody to take a look at the crater.

Only real casualty was the telegraph pole. The wires were severed and I would have to report it, but it was far preferable to any of us going in similar fashion.

It was all too much for the tractor driver. The churns had been packed with one hundred pounds of am-monium nitrate each, with fuel and oil and a booster and the poor man was left to reflect on what effect that little lot would have had on him. No way was he going to cut any more hedges that day and who could blame him as he set off back to his depot.

During the drive back to camp I held my own private post mortem on the operation. There was no doubt about it. I had made basic mistakes, some of which could have got me killed.

I would learn from these and I decided that God had been good to me and it was simply not my turn to go that day.

It was this incident that made me completely fatalistic about life and believe that if it was my turn to go then there was nothing I could do about it. And I have continued to hold that belief ever since.

I noticed, during the journey back, that my hands were stinging. I had not noticed it before, but now when I looked down, I found that my hands and fingers were bleeding from my forays into the gorse and brambles.

It was my first task and I had been well and truly blooded.

CHAPTER 6

£10,000 To Kill A Soldier

I SMILED as I entered our team's rest room and saw one of the lads fixing a familiar object to the wall. It was the twisted lid of one of the milk churns with which I had done battle just a short time ago and it was being solemnly secured among the myriad bits of paraphernalia that adorned the walls.

The majority of these were car number plates from the various jobs that the teams had tackled and as I watched a label was duly attached below the lid, recording the job, time, place and, most important, the name of the operator. "Fame at last!" I thought.

This, I realised, was Standard Operating Procedure to the boys on the team and wherever we went, they always brought back a memento.

As I had made my report to the watch keeper in the ops room when we got back to base, it was all done in a very matter-of-fact way. He had no way of knowing how satisfied I felt at having safely—well, almost safely— disposed of nearly 300lb of explosive. But the mood changed when a sartorially-elegant figure suddenly strode in. Major Faulkner was the Battalion ops officer and he really cut a dash in a natty pair of riding breeches. The Lancers' officers had brought their horses with them, would you believe, and the Galloping Major had been out in the saddle. Funny people, these cavalry!

But he had heard what I had been up to: "Well done, Felix!" he nodded, using the nickname that became attached to us due to our similarity, when waddling-about in our bomb suits, to the cartoon cat trudging off at the end of each film.

"Bloody well done!" I thought as I thanked him.

It was nice to be appreciated, but just how much my success meant to the battalion was only brought home to me in the mess later. Everybody, but everybody, it seemed, had all the details of the job and they all wanted to congratulate me—and buy me a drink. If I had accepted all the drinks I had been offered that night I would have been drunk as a skunk, but as I fought off yet another attempt to "buy me one" I explained my seeming lack of appreciation of their hospitality:

"But I don't drink! I tried to explain.

"Well try this then", insisted one persistent bloke.

"What is it?" I asked peering at what looked like a glass of fizzy water with a piece of lemon in it."

"Try it." For the sake of argument I did so, and to my surprise found the taste to my liking.

"That's nice. What is it?" I frowned.

"G and T"

"What?"

"Gin and tonic".

Well, I was still on duty, but I had another slurp to make sure of the taste—and marked it down for future reference. That was something else I had to thank these cavalrymen for.

After a while, I began to realise that the bomb had probably been laid to trap these lads and I had removed the hidden menace, which was why they were so grateful and jubilant. A good number of them would have perished if they had walked into that little lot.

Of course, I was pleased about it too, but now that the adrenalin had stopped pumping I was still surprised at their enthusiasm; to them it was very special. To me it was just part of my job and to this day I have never been able to reconcile the two different reactions to such events.

The happiness on the base had only just had time to subside when I was off again, with a terse set of instructions: 'Abandoned van seen in field after being chased previous night. Go by helicopter'.

There was disappointment among my loyal team, when they realised they would not be going along. The chopper concerned was a Sioux and carried only one passenger, which meant I could take the minimum of equipment.

Helicopters were a common sight in the Province, indeed they still are, with the landing pad at Bessbrook Mill claiming to be Europe's busiest heli-port—but for me it was another new experience.

As we soared off I found myself in a whole new world. I was amazed at what could be seen with such a bird's eye view—a realisation that was to stand me in good stead over the coming years as I surveyed various suspicious incidents. I also felt extremely vulnerable in the little plastic bubble that was the cockpit, but I quickly forgot my fears when I remembered the task. Blimey, yes, the task! Quickly, I fixed my mind on it—a possible car bomb, one of the trickiest tasks of them all in those early days.

And as I glanced down, there it was waiting for me, some 150 yards into a muddy field, with the cordon of troops in position. I got the pilot, Sergeant Dave Gibbs, to circle it as I anxiously surveyed the scene through binoculars. Then, we landed and I got out, deep in thought—

and nearly pulled my ears off as the headphones pulled me back with a jolt!

That was my first mistake. My second was to keep referring to the patrol leader, a sergeant, as "Staff". This was because he sported a crown about his stripes and in the RAOC that signified a staff sergeant. But not in the cavalry. I learned that his insignia of rank meant that he was a colour sergeant. Funny people, these cavalry!

The colour sergeant was accompanied by a plain clothes RUC constable who gave me what details he could. He had been up to the van, a Ford Anglia, he said, but had not tried to open it.

I gave thanks for that. "That's very wise," I told him grimly for his future reference, mindful of the horrendous possible consequences of such curiosity.

Carefully, I assessed the situation: what would be the target for a bomb? What did they hope to gain by planting one here? Was it a "come-on?" It was certainly not a good spot for an ambush and the troops had been here for hours without incident anyway.

While I systematically went through my procedure I suddenly realised how hungry I was. God, I'd missed lunch, while my pilot Dave, had nipped off to the nearest heli-pad, to refuel, he said—but the crafty sod had gone for his nosh and left me to call him when ready.

Lesson No. 1 Kevin, I thought: lay in a stock of Mars bars and always carry a flask. This bomb disposal busi-ness was hungry and thirsty work! But it was as if the staff—or rather colour—sergeant had been reading my mind. He produced a cup of tea for me and I learned they carried all the makings in the back of their vehicles. Good lads these cavalry!

I determined that I was not going to take any more risks than were necessary and would not detain the troops in the area a moment longer than was needed.

They had already been there several hours and I decided to destroy the vehicle in situ.

Using a Ferret scout car as cover, I attempted to shoot out the rear windows of the van with a shotgun, so that I could place an explosive charge inside it. But after three attempts it was clear that at this range of about 150 metres, a more accurate weapon was called for.

My eyes lighted on the .30 machine gun mounted on the scout car. "Sergeant, when did you last zero your machine gun?" I asked.

"Just last week, Felix" he said, his eyes lighting up with anticipation.

"Can you break a window in the van for me?"

"You bet your life I can!" he answered gleefully.

But before turning him loose with his toy I had to make a few checks. The only trouble with .30 high velocity ammunition is that it can travel a long way and I perused my map to see what buildings were in the area.

The only one was a school. It was about half a mile away and a long way out of the firing line, but I thought I ought to warn them and drove off there by Landrover, telling the headmistress there would be a couple of bangs and a small explosion.

I had asked her to keep the kids away from the windows, and they must have been made well aware of what was going on, because when I turned the happy machine gunner loose the crack! crack! of the weapon was greeted by loud cheers. It seemed we had an audience! Two small holes had appeared in one of the windows. "Again!" I shouted. Two more cracks. Two more holes. Another round of cheers—but the window remained stubbornly in place. Clearly, the weapon was too powerful and the bullets were going through too cleanly to shatter the glass.

"Sod this," I thought. More extreme measures were called for. Ankle deep in mud, I squelched up to the van.

The four bullet holes looked just like those stick-on ones you could get from filling stations at that time—and still the glass refused to budge when I tried it. There was only one thing for it. Down on my knees into the mud I went, fixing a charge on to the back axle before retiring gracefully and firing the charge.

Bang! The car split open to cheers from our nearby audience again. Clearly, it had not been a car bomb. I handed over to the RUC and we flew back over the school to complete their day of excitement.

Another day, another job. And now I had done a car successfully, which was a real feather in my cap. A car .... "Oh shit!" I realised with horror that I had not collected the coveted trophy and knew that the first thing the lads would ask me for would be a number plate. "They'll kill me", I thought ruefully.

Sure enough, they gave me hell. "Sorry lads" was all I could say, and stood there shamefaced as they put a label on the wall with the relevant details, and left a space above it. I never let them down again.

I was beginning to feel very much part of the scene now. I had been thrown in at the deep end without the supervision of a senior man to see me through and I had achieved success each time I had been called out. More important: I had survived.

But one of the incidents that earned me some real kudos within the somewhat upper-crust circle of the cavalrymen involved a particularly nasty weapon—the notorious Russian-made RPG-7 which, to the layman, is a 'rocket launcher'.

This was one of the best, if not the best, type of anti-tank weapons of its time. It fires an 84mm rocket-propelled grenade up to 500 metres and its shaped explosive charge will penetrate twelve inches of armour plate, squirting hot gas and molten armour into the interior. If it hits a human target it will of course, virtually vapourise it.

It was one of these particularly anti-social bits of kit that the IRA used during a five-man attack on the police station at Belleek, an incident which developed into a furious firefight. Sadly, an RUC constable was killed when an RPG missile hit a window of the station, a colour sergeant from the 16th/5th just escaping the blast.

I had to investigate this attack, one of several made during the day using weapons of this type. It was clear from the hole it had made that it was a hollow-charge type anti-tank weapon and I was glad of the information I had been able to glean when, the following morning I was summoned to 'prayers'—the Battalion's daily briefing and the Colonel put me on the spot by asking me what could be done to counteract such a weapon.

A tricky one indeed, but as the weapon was operated on the over pressure principle I gave my advice on how the various armoured vehicles could best be prepared for operations to give the crews the highest possible chance of surviving a hit.

Twenty four hours later, a signal came in from HQ that in the light of several RPG-7 attacks vehicles should be prepared in just the way I had already advised our detachment.

From then on I found that the Lancers treated me—to them just a young sergeant from outside their closely-knit circle of cavalrymen—with a good deal more respect, and they sought my advice frequently about their various ops.

A cavalryman I would never be, but it was clear that I had earned my spurs!

Life proceeded at a hectic pace and I had to tackle a non-stop variety of jobs to try to protect people and property. It was clear that the terrorists would stop at nothing in their murderous campaign. And if we needed any reminder of just how ruthless they were it came when a car bomb exploded outside a bar in Belfast, killing two little girls, aged six and four, who had been playing some 40 yards away.

In the same area explosives were found in carrier bags which had been placed by a pram in which a young baby was sleeping, a warning arriving only after the device had been discovered, then, a 14-year-old boy, who had just recovered from polio, was shot dead while on his way to school in his father's car.

These were the type of people we were up against. These incidents happened outside my area, but I was getting plenty of first-hand experience of the terrorist groups in my own neck of the woods.

In one period of five days it seemed I was never "home". Off I went to tackle the milk churns, the Ford Anglia van, a suspect car, which I opened up with one round from a Carl Gustav anti-tank weapon, a claymore mine which had exploded and injured two soldiers at Knockadoot Spring, and bombs in two pubs.

The first of the pub incidents ended quite cheerfully for us. Two armed men had left an old radio set on the end of the bar in Patrick Montague's pub in Beragh. It looked just the part, as it lay there among the pints of beer, as though it was there to entertain the customers—but inside lurked 15-20lb of explosive. A crack had been heard, which to me indicated that the detonator had gone off, but I was not quite sure that it was as harmless as it appeared and destroyed it with a controlled explosion just to make sure. My explosion was a far different affair from the one intended and the glasses of beer still sat on the bar ready to be finished when the customers were allowed to return.

As for Pat Montague, well, he was as pleased as Punch

as the lounge had just been renovated and as we were leaving he presented us with several bottles of good cheer "For forensic evidence, lads," he explained with a wink.

Another local was left with a distinct impression that the RAOC possessed special powers when McAleer's Bar in Omagh became a target, three terrorists planting a suitcase which must have contained 50-100lb of explosive.

I didn't get a chance to tackle this one, because, when I questioned a witness who had seen the terrorists I asked: "What time was this?"

"Twelve minutes past 10", he replied with precision.

"How can you be sure?" I queried.

"Because when they came in they put it alongside of me and I looked up at the clock and it was twelve minutes past ten."

Fair enough. It was now twenty-five to eleven and with that I started getting my ear defenders out and said to him: "Well, if it's going to go off it'll go off any time now".

Just as I was fitting the second earplug there was an almighty explosion and the pub shook. When I looked down, the poor man was cowering on the floor. When he got shakily to his feet he looked at me in amazement: "Jesus!" he said "You're a clever man. You knew exactly when it was going to go off!"

I hadn't the heart to tell him they had been going off within 25 to 30 minutes for a very long time. I just allowed him to believe in my magic powers!

Our team was having a successful tour. As the incidents followed quickly in the wake of one another I saw more and more of the Scenes of Crimes Officers to whom we had to pass the various bits and pieces of tasks for evidence.

It was while I was handing over another pile of bits after another successful operation that one of them said to me: "Hey, ATO, if you go on like this they're going to be putting the price up!"

"I looked at him, mystified: "What price?" I frowned.

"For you!" he laughed.

I still did not follow him, but when he explained, his answer stopped me in my tracks.

"What are you on about?"

"They will be putting the price up for you if you are any more successful – the terrorists! You don't think they all do this sort of thing for love of Ireland do you? They get paid for doing these jobs."

The light of realisation dawned on me with a feeling of horror as he explained that the bloke who made the bomb was not the one who laid it and that they paid somebody for taking the risk and that there would be a price for a successful operation – particularly if they nailed an ATO.

Stunned, I began to make a few inquiries and learned that for killing a bomb disposal operator the successful bomber would be paid an extremely high "bounty".

"How much?" I asked. Just how much was my life worth! This was a difficult one to get a first-hand answer on, as I could hardly walk into the nearest IRA staff meeting and ask! But the price that was generally bandied about was £10,000 – and at that time that was a hell of a lot of money. Not only that, it was part of the folklore that it remained the "target price" for life.

So, suddenly, all my successful ops against the IRA had left me with a price on my head. This was becoming a bit personal! I had never thought of it in that way before. It had just been my job, but from then on I realised that if I slipped up and saw the Big White Light some bloke would be spending his new-found riches in the pub that night and toasting my demise.

This was brought home to me with horrible suddenness one day when I heard that one of our sergeants from Lurgan had been killed.

Six or seven mortars had landed around the barracks at Lurgan. Now, one of the prime tasks when this occurs is to find the baseplate from where the missiles were fired. The terrorists had a habit of booby trapping these, but this was not what had caused the death of the sergeant. One of the missiles had misfired and was hanging out of the tube when he investigated and in the course of his task it had exploded, killing him instantly. It gave me a sick feeling when I learned that the top of his head had been taken clean off and that had a beret been put on him it woud have been impossible to tell anything was wrong with the poor lad.

That filled me with sadness and revulsion — but when I realised that some bastard would now be a good deal richer it made me mad. The bomber would probably receive considerably more cash than the ATO's dependants.

Because of the death of my colleague I had to take his place on a couple of tasks. It was standard practice and part of folklore, superstition, call it what you like, that we did not do somebody else's job unless there was no alternative, because if something happened to somebody deputising for you, there could be a feeling that maybe you would have done the job differently, and you would be left feeling responsible for the death of a colleague.

These thoughts were in my mind as I was called to Lurgan for a job that was outside my area. I didn't like it, for the reasons stated, but somebody had to do it — and that somebody was me.

This time the "present" awaiting me was a cardboard box inside a carrier bag that had been placed in the manager's office in an egg-packing plant in Coalisland.

When the security forces had investigated they had been attacked with small arms fire and mortars. This was an obvious lure to get them into the area, but even so, no way was I going to simply walk through the door to have a look. Having weighed up the situation I decided the window would do nicely for me.

This seemed like an easy thing to do—but the way I approached it gave the support team a nasty moment!

Opening a possibly booby-trapped window would not be the brightest thing to do, I thought, and decided to put my "TV knowledge" to good use. I had seen heroes smashing windows on TV with the barrels of their guns—and decided to do the same. But the glass they use on films is obviously not the same as that used in real life, and two heavy blows from my Browning pistol made no impression whatsoever. There was nothing for it, but to shoot the window out, so cocking the weapon I did just that, without thinking to warn anybody, and until I was able to shout that it was "Only me!" or words to that effect, the troops thought they were under fire again!

Cursing my thoughtlessness, I clambered in and disrupted what turned out to be a box of sand and soil—as we had thought, just another "come-on".

Come on, false alarm or a bomb, they are all the same to us and you sweat the same sweat whatever it is. I was glad to have got away with safely dealing with another man's task, but it gave me an uneasy feeling in doing so.

Now that the job had become personal between me and the terrorists, my attitude quickly changed and became a great deal more hardened.

Now, the deadly game had a more sinister theme to it and I thought grimly to myself: "Right, you buggers, you are not going to beat me!"

It was quite in order to destroy something where it was if that was the best and safest way to do it, and a bomb could be quite a blessing for a shopkeeper if his business was not going too well. Destruction of his premises, compensation and a new start elsewhere, could come in handy at times, but I was determined now that the bombers were not going to cost the crown a penny more than was absolutely necessary.

It was said, in those days, that every time an ATO went out he saved the Government £80,000. They reckoned that if we had to blow up a car—one of our trickiest tasks in those days—but we saved a building from going up by defusing a bomb there, it was losing a couple of thousand pounds on the car while saving possibly more than a million pounds on the building. Not a bad cost-effectiveness!

When I thought about it, I realised that soldiers got compensation for injuries on a rising scale, so it made sense that the bounty hunters would also be getting paid for their dirty work.

So now I had become a prime target. I was being stalked by the faceless cowards who spoke about being "soldiers" but did not have the guts to face our lads as soldiers would.

But without knowing it, they had done me a favour. Now I had learned what the dirty game was really about, it only made me doubly determined to come out of it a winner.

CHAPTER 7

The Poisoned Dwarf

THE rain was bucketing down as I stood, ankle-deep in an icy stream beside the culvert—and breathed in the unmistakable odour of nitrobenzene.

It was coming from fourteen plastic sacks of home-made explosive, which had been crammed into the culvert, which was some two-foot six in diameter. Northern Ireland is riddled with culverts and they quickly became favourite places for hiding explosives, with the intention of causing, via command wire, an explosion when the intended target passed overhead. At times it was, and sadly still is to this day, a highly-effective way of causing considerable mayhem.

This time, however, an alert soldier has smelled the filthy stuff as he and his mates carefully carried out an inch-by-inch search of the ground around a bread van, which had been hijacked, then abandoned, with the tyres shot out so that it could not easily be moved.

It was alleged to have a bomb on board, but we had no way of knowing, until we took a closer look, where there really was one, or whether it was another of the terrorists' 'come-ons', to lure troops into the area, then attempt to blow them up. That was something we had to discover by treading very carefully.

As the planned clearance of the area proceeded, I sat in the back of an APC with my team while the troops did their search on what was a typical Northern Ireland day: it was peeing down!

Suddenly, there was a shout as one of the team made the find and the vehicle went backwards very rapidly out of the immediate danger area. Now, it was up to me and I clambered out to get a taste of the local weather as I gingerly took a closer look. I was soon as soaked as the search team as I sloshed about in the stream with the freezing rain trickling steadily down my neck.

I knew the device was not light sensitive as the lad who had made the find had shone a torch into the culvert, so the thing to do was to find the command wire. As I scrabbled about in the icy water, I suddenly scooped up the wire—and promptly dropped it with shock. The IRA had an unfriendly habit of booby-trapping the wires themselves, but this one had not gone off, so I tugged at it and discovered that it ran along an earth bank. We later discovered that it ran for about 800 metres in all, but for now, some 60 metres down the wire, I got everybody down for safety, then cut one wire—we never cut both at once as this procedure had caused the death of one of our men and was one of the hard lessons we had learned.

So far so good. Now for the sacks—and this was going to be difficult. Back into the freezing stream I went, having to crouch to get a grip on the nearest sack.

By now my clothes were a sodden mess and to make matters worse I was wearing a brand new set of denims, which were hard to come by and highly-prized items of kit at that time. They were going through a rigorous on-site testing, of that there was no doubt!

I managed to get a hook and line around a couple of

bags and wrestle them clear of the culvert. They were linked by Cordtex and contained half to three quarters of a hundredweight each of ammonium nitrate fuel oil and nitrobenzene. Half a dozen bags later it was getting more and more difficult to get at the damned things. How the hell had the terrorists got them in there? I am only a small man, but I just could not get at the remaining bags and began to think perhaps the IRA had a midget in their ranks.

In desperation I went round to the other side of the culvert. Suddenly, I had a brainwave: I would build a dam! The team may have thought that some of the water had got into my brain, but they jumped into the stream with me and like gang of schoolkids we piled mud and stones together on the upstream side of the culvert until we had our dam built to the necessary specifications. The intention was to release the water from the dam in the hope that the force of water would dislodge the bags.

We must have looked a right lot of nutters, uniformed soldiers, playing about with rocks and mud in a stream in the pouring rain, but, daft or not, when we finally let the water go and rushed eagerly to the other side, to our delight, out came the bags in a tremendous cascade of floodwater and I breathed a sigh of relief.

The 14 sacks were found to contain 700lb of explosive — and this meant that our team had made the record books: it was the largest mine discovered in the Province and the Lancers' magazine later suggested, somewhat tongue-in-cheek, that the find should be included in the Guinness Book of Records.

There was so much explosive to dispose of that we split it into three piles, then blew it all over the local farmer's fields. It was a quick way of spreading some free fertilizer for him, but the ungrateful so-and-so did not appreciate the gesture. The cheeky bugger attempted to sue the

Army for the three holes we had made in his fields! But it was here that Army diplomacy won the day: he got nothing for the damage to his precious fields — and we did not charge him for all the free fertilizer!

Having disposed, at last, of the explosives, I was still faced with the possibility of more "presents" in the bread van, which had been dumped by four men, near Rosslea. A box, which they claimed to be a bomb, had been thrown in the back, but, as I had guessed, this turned out to be a hoax. There was nothing in the van to worry us, it was just a lure to get troops to pass over the culvert.

We had been at it for several hours, I was soaked to the skin and absolutely knackered, but at last I thought, I could go home and get out of my wet things. Wrong! My eyelids were drooping with fatigue as I flew back in the helicopter when a message came over the radio diverting us to another job. A sack had been spotted in a ditch at the side of a road and there was a report of the old familiar smell again from another nearby culvert. "Here we go again!" I thought grimly.

But this time, my worst fears, with the struggle with the fourteen sacks fresh in my mind, were groundless. There were seven sacks, of the usual mixture, in the culvert, but the job was not complete. There was no timing device or command wire. This was just a "find" of a bomb in the making — the sacks came out this time without any trouble and I destroyed them in an adjacent field, breaking four windows in the nearby rectory at Lisnaskea, I later learned.

That brought my total for the day to 820lb of explosive destroyed and I had good reason to be satisfied with my day's work, but the only thing on my mind was a bath, some grub and some kip — in that order.

On the way back, however, something else began to occupy my attention. One of my hands was beginning to ache quite badly and I noticd it was covered with thorn cuts. The nitro had obviously got into the wounds; it would have been difficult for it not to have done. I stank of the bloody stuff. It was all over my new pullover and much-prized trousers (lightweight) as the Army called them. By the time we landed the hand was giving me considerable discomfort, so I put off the urgent call for a bath and tea, my favourite meal of the day, had a quick wash and went to see the Medical Officer.

The Doc listened to my tale of woe, had a quick look at my hand, then asked what the smell was.

"Nitrobenzene," I replied.

He walked across to a curtained-off corner, where I could hear him rifling through a book.

"What was it again?" he called.

"Nitrobenzene."

"Right. Get your clothes off!" he commanded, emerging from behind his curtain.

Blimey! What was going on? I'd heard of doctors like this, but I hadn't expected to find one in the Army!

"But Doc," I protested "I've only got a thorn in my hand!"

"Get your clothes off!" came the repeated command.

"But I've had no tea!" I wailed, desperate to protect my modesty.

"Get 'em off!"

"What's going on?" I demanded.

"You've probably got nitrobenzene poisoning," he explained somewhat to me relief.

I had not been aware it was a dangerous substance, in that sense, but the Doc left me in no doubt as he nodded towards my heap of crumpled clothes.

"Get them burned!" I was stunned to hear him say.

I was mortified. "What? These are new!" I protested,

having been issued with them only two days earlier. But there was no moving him.

"Doesn't matter," he said sternly "We can't have them around."

I soon discovered that he wasn't joking and that there was no way, either, I was going to escape to the mess.

"You can't .... I'm on duty," I whinged "I'm here all the time".

"No arguments," he shook his head: "I'm bedding you down for observation."

All my wittering about not having eaten was to no avail. "We'll get you fed," he promised, then removed the thorn, dressed my hand and ordered me into bed after I had taken a shower.

Then came the next in a series of events that had taken me by surprise: "Are you thirsty?" asked my captor.

I jumped swiftly, ever mindful of the absence of food and drink: "Yes, of course I am. I've had no tea" I reminded him for the umpteenth time.

"We'll get you some tea," he promised again, "But have you got a dry throat?"

"Well yes," I persisted "I'm thirsty."

"Well, I'm going to give you an injection," he said "And you tell me if you get a dry throat."

"I am thirsty," I tried again.

"No," he said "I really mean a dry throat."

With that he gave me an injection. "What is it?" I asked. "Atropine."

My basic military knowledge told me that this was a neutralizing agent for nerve gas, but I soon learned what he meant by a dry throat.

In no time at all my throat was on fire! It was as though it had been lined with sandpaper. I learned that when this is administered, if you haven't got nerve agent poisoning, or, in my case, nitrobenzene poisoning, and you are given atropine, you suffer from atropine poisoning, which, apparently, is quite controllable and nothing to really get bothered about.

Well, I suppose I should have been relieved that all was well, from the medic's point of view, but my throat was something else! I was kept in for 24 hours and had to inform HQ at Lisburn that I was hors de combat for the time being — but at least, and at long last, an orderly brought me some tea across from the mess. As for my sadly-lamented kit, the Doc promised to arrange for a new set to be issued to me.

What a day! I had destroyed 820lb of explosive that could have caused God-knows what atrocities; I had had my best kit destroyed — and I'd been poisoned, all in one day, and I'd only been there a few weeks.

When my team heard I was in dock they came across to see me. They were extremely annoyed at not being taken on the job with me as a unit. Only one had been allowed to accompany me as I had had to go by helicopter, but if they had known the way I felt for several hours they would have realised that their envy was very much misplaced.

Over the years, as a little guy, on the odd occasion when I had attempted to hit back at my invariably bigger detractors when they had tried to take a rise out of me, if I'd come up with some particularly evil way of getting back at them, I had, like most little men in the same situation, been labelled "The poisoned dwarf." It was all part of the process of learning to put up with the insults that frequently come the way of us "shorties" — but this was the first time in my life they could legitimately have claimed that their eagerly-applied epithet was true!

I had ample time to get over my discomfort, as things slowed right down for a while, then came the most unpleasant incident in which I had been involved to date.

An RUC reserve constable was killed when his car blew up as he reversed it after coming off duty. He had been caught in a classic terrorists' ploy: they had put a movement or release-type pressure switch behind a back wheel of his car, knowing he had to reverse it, and when he had done so he had been killed instantly. It was a stunning shock for the colleague who had been sitting in the car with him while he warmed up the vehicle, before walking some twenty yards to his van. As he had reached it, his mate's car had been blown to bits by a bomb of around 20-50lb.

It frightened the poor man so much that he would not get into his van in case that was booby-trapped too. We had to go down and investigate it for him, but though we explosively opened it, just to be on the safe side, there was nothing in it. His friend had been the target. The remains of the car were taken away that day, but we had to return the next morning to check the area—and ended up wishing we hadn't. Suddenly, one of the team happened to look up, and there, hanging in a tree, was a piece of the murdered man's hand. It had not been seen by the clearance team and it gave me one of those jolts that turn your stomach.

I had always been aware that there were good and bad sections in almost any community, but this brought it home to me with a sickening feeling just what sort of barbarians we were up against over here. By now I was well and truly immersed in the deadly "game," though I could well have done without this latest introduction to another facet of it.

I was daily learning these things, hard facts in the life-or-death struggle in which we were all engaged.

One fact I had learned very quickly was that in Northern Ireland everybody believes they are a target and when the wife of a REME coporal received a package from

Enniskillen, from an address she did not recognise, she immediately gave us a call.

Wearing my armoured suit, just in case, I carefully slit open the suspect package—and found myself staring at a pin cushion in the form of an imitation sliced orange! It turned out that the lady who had previously lived at the address had made dolls and soft furnishings and had sent the present to the new tenant.

A happy end to what had looked sinister to one frightened lady, but the next day another incident had the whole joint jumping!

A box, with wires protruding from it ominously, was discovered on the steps of the CO's house in Lisanelly Barracks. Panic! Now they were after the Old Man himself! I shot down there to deal with the "device"—and you could hear the sighs of relief when I discovered that the "bomb" was nothing more than a telephone engineer's testing meter, which he had forgotten the day before. We were all relieved, but I hoped that somebody made sure that the prat concerned was given a heavy reminder to have just a little more thought to where he left his equipment in future. We had enough on our plates dealing with real devices and malicious hoaxes without having to shred our nerves because somebody had an aptitude for selecting one of the most strategic targets in the camp when he decided to switch his brain to neutral.

CHAPTER 8

Double Trouble

TIME began to fly by as the incidents came thick and fast. It certainly kept us on our toes, but I was well into my tour now and while I was kept busy the time was slipping by that much faster.

I was called out to several jobs in rapid succession during a period of intense activity. Two claymore-type devices, which have a "shotgun" effect, went off just 50 yards in front of a patrol who were doing a road clearance—but they were lucky. A man carrying a battery had been seen in the area, but if he had set it off, his timing was out as none of the soldiers was hurt. I had to take a look at the scene of the incident, then we received a call to the Border, where a suspicious sack had been left under a bridge. I destroyed the sack, which turned out to be harmless—and in doing so endeared myself to a bunch of squaddies. The explosion took the keystone out of the bridge on which there had been a permanent vehicle check point, but when the bridge collapsed with the removal of the stone, the VCP had to go with it—to the great glee of the lads tasked with this somewhat mundane of jobs.

An eagle-eyed soldier spotted another suspicious bag in the entrance to a culvert—a favourite place, as I had already discovered at the cost of considerable pain and discomfort, for planting bombs. I flew down expecting the worst after my previous experience. It turned out to be a plastic bag of the type workmen used to protect the wooden supports of the culverts while they were being constructed, but it was a great "spot" by the lads and showed they were on the ball.

Another claymore went off with no obvious target in the vicinity. We concluded that perhaps Paddy had got fed up waiting in the rain and fired it anyway, then gone off to the pub. It was to be hoped he wasn't heading for the Dearg Valley Hotel. For three of his mates, masked and shouting that there was a bomb with an anti-handling device, had run in and caused terror to the customers by planting a device which later exploded before we could get to it. It did considerable damage and must have contained between 50 and 100lb of explosive.

Intespersed with all this hectic activity were spells of inactivity that could easily have become boring if you did not have something to occupy your mind. My favourite pastime led me to the company of the Army Air Corps, that elite little band of lads in the light blue berets who are the kings of the air in their helicopters.

It was they who taught me the old Royal Navy game of uckers, which is similar to ludo—though you must never call it that—and is taken extremely seriously, and I was soon a regular member of their school.

But in those days we were allowed to take some of our leisure time outside the barracks. It would be unthinkable nowadays, when you couldn't be expected to remain safe for very long, but in the early 70s soldiers were familiar figures as they sought entertainment away from camp. Our team were no different from the rest, especially when we got to know of the Silver Birches. This was, officially, a hotel, but it was definitely not the place you would pick to take a lady on a night out if you wanted to impress her. It wasn't exactly spit and sawdust—but that was probably because the sawdust had been swept up before opening time! But beggars cannot be choosers. It was only about 40 yards from the front gate of the barracks across the street, and that made it the "in" place as far as we were concerned, especially as there was a bit of dance floor, where they held a disco.

I went across there several times, always with Graham, my escort, at my side, and both of us armed with nine-millimetre Brownings, just to be on the safe side. The talent was in good order there, and friendly enough, but one night a young colleen with whom I had quite a few dances, suddenly began to show a little too much interest in me for my liking.

The twist was all the rage then, but near the end of the evening, there came a slow, smoochy-type number. The girl had her arms around me in the normal way and I thought nothing of it until I was suddenly aware that her hands were roaming over my lower back—and around the waistband where my automatic was stashed. I had the distinct feeling she was "fishing". It was obvious to a blind man, with our English accents and short haircuts and the barracks just across the street, that we were soldiers, but this young lady was taking a bit of an unhealthy interest all of a sudden.

My suspicions were confirmed when she asked: "Are you carryin'?"

"What me? No love," I said as lightly as I could "No, no." With that I thanked her for the dance and went back to my seat. Perhaps I should have taken notice of it, but I didn't and after a couple of gin and tonics I needed a pee.

"Just going for a leak," I told Graham.

I was standing there doing what comes naturally after a drink or three when I heard the door open. Glancing over my shoulder I saw two large Paddies I had not seen before, approaching the stalls. There was nobody else in

83

there and plenty of stalls, but these two stood one either side of me saying nothing to each other, or me.

The hairs on the back of my neck began to stand up. Suddenly, I was stuck between two big Irishmen without any back-up whatsoever. The Browning in my waistband was beginning to burn a hole in my back. I was forming the definite impression that I might need it before many more seconds had passed, yet when you have your old man in your hands, sliding one away and up to where your other weapon is concealed is not the easiest thing in the world to accomplish surreptitiously!

It was around this time that one of the most horrific incidents happened that made it clear that it was becoming unsafe to venture out when we were not on duty. Four senior NCOs had been lured by girls and then murdered by terrorists. The possibility of a similar situation developing flashed into my head and with these more important thoughts the need to pass water ceased abruptly. I had the feeling these two were about to jump me any second and I vowed to myself that I would fight them off to the best of my ability. If I could get my hand on my pistol in time I would have no qualms about using it if I had to. The seconds seemed to drag by as I waited for them to make their move. I tried to stay calm, ready to fight for my life.

Just then, the decision was taken out of my hands when the door swung open and a familiar voice called: "All right, Boss?" It was Graham, God bless him. The cavalry had arrived in the nick of time!

A wave of relief swept over me. And my "friends" changed just as quickly. The men who had been standing silently either side of me, suddenly lost their air of menace as they found their tongues and became chatty, asking us: "Sure, are ye having a good time, boys?"

Yes, we were having a great time, we assured them.

This was a great place and we were enjoying every minute of it, and hadn't the weather been lovely for the time of year? I played for time and waited for them to leave, then: "Right: back to camp!" I snapped.

"But Boss," wailed my escort "I'm just chatting to this bird..."

Sorry, back to camp!" I said firmly.

Back we went. There was no sign of our new-found friends by now, but I reported the incident as soon as we got back.

Neither of us were much help when we were asked for descriptions of the pair, I'm afraid. They all tended to look the same to me, and I had had my mind on being ready to take action had the need arisen, rather than forming an acute mental picture of them.

The incident scared the wits out of me and served as a warning. We eased off on the Silver Birches, and Graham and I made sure we were together at all times when we went out. He never left my side again—particularly when I went for a pee!

As if I needed a reminder of to what depths the terrorists would sink, I received one with one of the most sickening and heartrending acts of stupid slaughter I had come across when yet another car bomb exploded without warning in Killeter. It killed a teenage girl, Kathleen Dolan and if that was not bad enough, by the cruellest twist of fate, it was the fact that she was out posting invitations for her forthcoming wedding that led to her death, right opposite her father's pub. Two of the poor girl's younger sisters, who had been helping prepare the invitations in their home across the road, were also injured, but not too seriously.

The following day I had to examine the area, and the full horror of the murder was brought home to me when I peered at the wall beside the post box opposite the pub. I could see something there, but wasn't sure what—then I realised I was looking at the shape of the young girl where she had been blown by the blast, before being buried under rubble. There were hairs still stuck to the brickwork and the shape was plain to see. It was thought that the 50lb bomb had been placed there as revenge for the killing of part-time UDR soldier William Bogle, who had been shot in the back and killed just a few feet away while out shopping with his family.

Just two more helpless victims of the sheer mindless stupidity of this senseless so-called "war" that was going on. It made me feel terribly sad at the needless loss of another young life. A few days later the one thousand or so people who attended the girl's funeral were called upon by the priest not to hold any bitterness or rancour for the "misguided individuals" who had planted the bomb, but to have pity and forgiveness for them. I reckon that must have been a difficult view for the bereaved to accept.

Nobody wanted to talk to the security forces about this incident, and it was perfectly understandable and when the call came, the same day of this murder, that a Vauxhall Viva, which had been used in the planting of the bomb, had been found in the entrance to a farmyard, I didn't mess about and totally destroyed it where it was—keeping the ritual number plate, of course.

A second car which had been used in the incident, this time an Austin Cambridge, was found abandoned on the road to Killeen. It too, met with a similar fate. But we were too late to reach a Morris 1100 that had been left outside a garage in Omagh. It went up, thanks to to a charge of 50-100lb, though fortunately it did very little damage.

The car spread itself over an area of some 300 yards up and down the street and ended a day of the dreaded car bomb. But if that was the day of the car bomb there followed the day of the suitcase—a hell of a day of activity.

It began with a suitcase bomb being planted in a side passage near the toilets in Broderick's Bar in Omagh. This went off causing a great deal of damage. Then, a blue suitcase turned up in the middle of a street. A taxi driver who was going to dump it in the river several hundred yards away, changed his mind when he heard it ticking! Sensible man, that. We were getting our equipment ready to deal with it when it beat us to it and went off.

One incident followed another—a "bomb" in a holdall in a cement mixer, just for a bit of variation, turned out to be a hoax and was dealt with by a small charge, but there was nothing of a hoax about the stolen car, left outside a supermarket in Lisnaskeagh. A plastic bag on the back seat exploded, causing extensive damage to the area. That was a day we were glad to see the end of, though damage to property was always preferable to loss of life, or injury to people, the vast majority of whom were, and are, ordinary law-abiding folk.

A few days later, a device with a difference raised a smile. A Benson and Hedges cigarette packet, in a boutique, was found to contain a condom, filled with a mix of candle grease, sodium chlorate, and sugar in a solution of sulphuric acid. I hook and lined this out of the store and cut it open with secateurs. What a waste! But perhaps the would-be bomber was a good catholic boy and had no use for such items.

CHAPTER 9

Out With A Bang!

A S I listened to the story the RUC contable was telling me, I was becoming more and more annoyed. I had been called out to an incident in Bearagh, where a device had been planted by terrorists in Montague's Bar with a five-minute warning given. It was clearly a job for our special talents—but somebody, it appeared, had been doing my job for me—or trying to—and I was not the Army's happiest fella as the policeman related the details.

There had been an explosion, but there had been no damage to the pub. It appeared that three soldiers, accompanied by the policeman, had approached this device and one of the patrol had attached a rope to it and had then pulled it some 100 yards down a lane and fired one 7.62 round into it from his self-loading rifle, causing it to explode. The device contained, I reckoned, 10-20lb of the usual co-op mixture and it had slightly injured the marksman.

I arrived there late at night and got this tale out of the policeman, who admitted that the rope used by the bright spark from the infantry was about twenty to thirty yards long. Now when I get into a rage I am one of those people who literally go speechless, and by the time the reluctant limb of the law had unfolded all the details—or all those he was going to tell me—I was livid. I was beside myself with fury at the sheer stupidity of the people concerned.

For a few moments I was unable to speak, but when I recovered myself I let the poor constable have both barrels, and made it clear that I was going to crucify the soldier when I tracked him down! What the hell they were thinking of I couldn't imagine. It was the job of the RAOC experts to decide what to do with such devices, not cowboys with bits of rope who decided they were John Wayne. Apart from disturbing the device I couldn't believe that the bloody idiot would actually fire at it with his rifle! If anything was to be fired at it, I would have done so with a low velocity round, not the high-powered SLR, which would go through something and keep on going. I gave the policeman the bollocking of his life, then sought out the squaddie's OC and told him how lucky this lad was not to have got himself, and possibly the others with him, blown over several grid squares of the Province. If he wanted to get himself killed the IRA were out there waiting to oblige; he didn't have to do it for them!

Car bombs continued to be one of the favourite and most destructive devices of the terrorists and we had to investigate every suspicious circumstance in which a car had been stolen, often with widely differing results.

A Morris Minor Traveller was reported as having been left outside a hospital entrance for three days and when we discovered that the owner was away in England we decided to take a closer look at it. We hook and lined the doors and seats out of it until we were satisfied it was not booby-trapped—and gave it back to him in the condition in which he left it.

On New Year's Eve, the owner of a Capri 1600, a lieutenant in the UDR, was not so fortunate. His car was stolen and left near the racecourse in Enniskillen in a place where he was certain to see it on his way home—an obvious attempt to get him to go straight to it and get in, feeling relieved that it had turned up. But the police suspected an obvious booby-trap and we were called in. This car was only six months old and was a clear candidate for destruction where it stood. I hated the thought of doing this and explained to the poor lad the pros and cons of the situation; if he wanted to take the risk of opening it up, it was up to him, but if he got away in one piece it would be too good to be true.

He was too sensible a lad to take unnecessary risks and said, with an air of resignation: "No. Do what you have to do."

A day later the terrorists sent fraternal greetings to the occupants of Bearagh police station via an RPG that missed and went into a shop opposite that was, thankfully, unoccupied.

I was on my way to Lurgan, with my team, for a farewell drink with the OC there and as chance would have it, by being in the right place at the right time I was able to "steal" two tasks from my colleagues in that area. Now, we didn't like trespassing on anybody else's patch for the reasons stated, but while we were monitoring the radio we heard that there were two devices in the square at Dungannon. I radioed in that as I was only twenty minutes or so away could I help? What I meant was that I would go straight there and as I was outside my area I would do the preliminary ordnance reconnaissance work and take charge until the Lurgan team arrived. To my astonishment however, I was quickly tasked to them. What? This was not on, it was not my patch. Trust me to open my big mouth! Now, I had to overcome all the inbred superstitions about working on somebody else's patch.

But I just had to get on with it and we were off to a flying start, when the Police and Army personnel at the scene were amazed that the bombs and bullets boys could turn up so quickly.

In fact, we had arrived too quickly. Standard operating procedure demanded that all devices were left a certain length of time for safety before a manual approach was made, so I started questioning witnesses. while keeping an eye on my watch.

When I'd obtained all the information I needed I announced: "Hang on. I'm just off to check on something. I'll be back in a little while."

I left the rest of the team, who knew full well what I was up to, and walked round the corner to the RUC police station. It was Top of the Pops on television, so I sat with the police, brushing up my knowledge of all the latest pop songs for half an hour or so, then, when the cameras zoomed in on the twirling mini-skirts at the end of the show I strolled back round the corner into the square and said: "Right. Where were we?" and carried on with the job.

Bomb No. 1 was in a suitcase in a haberdashery shop. The second was in a cafe. I removed the first one with hook and line, slit open the top and found 20lb of co-op and 30lb of Gelamex inside, with a clock and battery in a one-gallon plastic container. I had cut the wires to the detonator and separated everything when I opened the plastic container, but my eyes fastened on the hand of the clock, which was a mere fraction from the wire!

It was such a shock that in a lightning reflex action I hurled the clock away, getting the firing switch as far away as possible. I watched it go bouncing down the street while I reflected that, yes, it was true: adrenalin WAS most definitely brown!

One down, one to go in a wave of relief .... and No. 2 immediately posed a problem as the owner of the shop could not be found, so we decided to shoot out the glass-fronted door with a shotgun. There was no cover in the square, so I borrowed an armoured Pig from the troops with the intention of approaching to within twenty or thirty yards, poking the shotgun through an observation slit and blasting away at the door. This may sound a safe routine, but it was very much in my mind that on an earlier tour somebody had been using a Pig in a similar manner to observe a device when it had gone off. It was so powerful that it had ripped the suspension off the vehicle. The ATO had been blinded in one eye, which was bad enough, but the photographer with him, who had been aiming his camera through a slit, had been killed when it had recoiled and struck him in the head.

I fired one round, saw that I had hit the window and fired twice more to make sure, then returned the Pig to its worried driver, who was sure it was about to be blown to bits.

I climbed out of the back door, satisfied with the way things had gone so far and was startled when one of my team cried "Christ Boss! What's the matter? What have you been doing?"

Only now, did I realise that I was covered in blood. My blood! I had been so busy concentrating, that I had not noticed the recoil from the weapon, which had struck me in the nose, making it bleed. It was a minor injury, but there was blood everywhere, enough to give the lads a scare.

The cafe bomb was in between two seats and contained about 25lb of explosive. I chopped the bag in two with a loop of explosive Cordtex, and was able to remove the contents using the good old hook and line.

Two devices on the way to a night out for a farewell drink. Not a bad spot of "overtime".

When we finally arrived at the party I was inundated

with questions from the resident team: "Well, what was it? How did you get on?"

They couldn't wait to hear the details. But were they pissed off when they realised I had stolen two "live" ones from right under their noses and had added them to my tally!

The previous year our teams had dealt with more than two thousand incidents in the Province and the way they were coming in now, it appeared we were well up with that rate.

We were spared one call, however, when a patrol caught six men who were carrying a milk churn, in which was 90lb of explosive. You had to give them full marks for trying. When challenged, one of them told the patrol leader: "Ah, sorr! There youse are. I'm glad we have found youse. We were just bringing this in. We've found it!"

It was a splendid "find" on their part and it earned them all long stretches for terrorism.

CHAPTER 10

The Dashing
White Sergeant

THERE were periods in Omagh when there was just
nothing to do once we had exhausted all our usual
pastimes. Nothing. In our corps they could not give
us other jobs to do in case we were needed for our usual
role, so the boys either practised yet again with our kit, or
played squash, while I went over to the Air Corps den in
search of another game of uckers.

But even this got boring after a while and as I eyed the
dashing cavalry officers going out on their horses I began
to fancy adding another string to my bow. I had, after all,
done some riding while stationed at Kineton, where I had
taken a farmer's horse out for a trot a time or two, so I
knew there was nothing to it. I was as good a Roy Rogers
as any of them. So, the next opportunity I had I button-
holed Major Faulkner, the ops officer, who I knew had
two horses with him, as any self-respecting cavalry officer
would.

"Mind if I have a ride sometime?" I asked boldly "Can I
exercise one of your horses for you?"

He seemed delighted at finding a kindred spirit among
the RAOC, "Can you ride?" he asked.

94

"Yes. I've ridden before," I nodded, as one equestrian gentleman to another.

"Fine. No problem," said the major, and with that he phoned his stables and informed them that when ATO turned up he was to be given free rein, so to speak, of one of the major's hunters.

"Great!" I thought. "I'm in," and two days later, during another slack spell I decided to keep him to his word.

I was eagerly looking forward to this new diversion, and duly turned up at the stables feeling very macho. I even had my pistol with me—just like they did in the films—but then I stopped in my tracks. Surely, the horse at which I was being pointed could not be mine? I gaped in awe. When your are 5ft. 4ins., anything over 5ft. 4 ins. is big, but this bloody animal standing before me was ginormous! I couldn't believe my eyes. It was a beautiful beast, no doubt about that, a light chestnut colour, but I had never seen anything so big before, it must have been 17 hands at the very least. It was so big that I couldn't even reach the stirrups and had to be given a leg up. But there was no turning back and once in position, with the horse standing beautifully still, I began to feel, literally, on top of the world. I breathed a sigh of relief as my trusty steed did as it was bid and turned and walked obediently exactly where I wanted it to.

I had already mapped out a route and off we went, nothing clever, just walking around the perimeter of the camp. "Nothing to this," I thought, "Can't imagine why I didn't think of it sooner," the horse and I were clearly well suited. This was the life, knew what they were doing these cavalry types, and now I was one of them. I was as pleased as Punch with myself. This was living in the most upper-crust style.

Before leaving I had told the ops room where I was going and when a helicopter flew over, I looked up to see the pilot signalling me to go back to camp. My ride was over, or so I thought with a sense of disappointment. Dutifully, I turned round and headed back. I had no sooner done so, than I realised my trusty steed knew it was going home and was in total agreement with the idea. I could feel it begin to quicken its pace immediately. Fair enough, I was clearly wanted in a hurry, so I gave it a quick "gee up", thinking a smart trot would do the trick. That was not good enough for the bloody horse however. Suddenly, it tore off down the grass verge like a rocket as if we were taking part in the Grand National.

"Whoa! Whoa!" I shouted in desperation, tugging with all my might at the reins. My efforts had no effect whatsoever. What had been an obedient, quiet beast had turned into a frightening, charging animal that was totally out of my control and going flat out.

We were going at a thundering gallop and I was petrified. The dashing white sergeant wasn't in it. There couldn't have been any colour left in my face, as I clung on desperately. Suddenly, as the camp gates loomed into sight, Red Rum left the grass verge and swung over at a perilous angle, hooves ringing on the hard surface, slipping all over the place as it headed for the gates, which were quickly becoming alarmingly close with no slackening in our speed.

The soldier on the gate eyed the strange sight curiously as the huge beast pounded towards him. He probably couldn't hear me under his helmet but I was shrieking at the top of my voice: "Open the gates! Open the fucking gates!"

Oh God! I realised it wasn't going to stop. The bloody thing was going to jump the barrier! Grimly I clung on like a limpet, resigned to my fate, then, at the last moment, horse and sentry realised all was not well; the sentry started to open the gates; the horse thought he

Right: Busiest heli-port in Europe. A Puma takes off with an underslung load, with a Wessex, Scout and (foreground) a Gazelle awaiting their turn.

Below: Happy snap: K.C., in bomb suit, posing with SLR while waiting to go out on a job.

Below (right): Mural on the wall of the bomb team's "home" in Bessbrook Mill, depicting Felix the cat. Photo: John Fox Manchester Evening News.

Left: The bomb disposal team follow a command wire from three gas cylinders each containing 20lb of homemade explosive.
Above: A command wire is followed across a stream, having been fed through a hosepipe.
Below: Present for the troops!. These three explosive-packed milk churns had been left where soldiers would have gathered at Gortin firing ranges. The command wires can be seen running from the necks of the churns.

Above: Bang! This is what just 1lb of high explosive can do to a car.
Left: You sweat the same sweat whether it's a real device or a false alarm . . . K.C. in full bomb suit at Lisanelly Barracks, Omagh, slits open a suspect package, which turned out to be a pin cushion!

Above: Pick up the bits somebody! This wagon contained six radio-controlled milk churn bombs. Shown after clearance, with six tons of dried fruit and more than 100 boxes of Weetabix scattered about the road.

Left: A hole in the side of a wagon, made explosively, by K.C., to gain access to three of six milk churns, which were packed with explosive.

Below (left): Two milk churns, which each contained 100lb of high explosve, after being pulled clear of the wagon.

Below (right): One of the milk churns with flatsword embedded.

Top: *Aerial view of hijacked tanker and truck on the Dublin to Dundalk road, seen from the South.*

Above: *Come into my parlour . . . Kevin Callaghan atop the hijacked tanker after dealing with the booby-trap device that was meant to give him an explosive "send-off".*

Right: *Kevin (centre) explains to members of the intelligence team, the make-up of the tanker device.*

Above: The tubes of death . . . nine out of ten mortars on launchers are still in place on a lorry ready to be fired at Newry Police Station.

Left: The sophisticated delay and firing device for the mortars aimed at Newry Police Station.

Below: This Mark Nine mortar tube contained 40lb of home-made explosive.

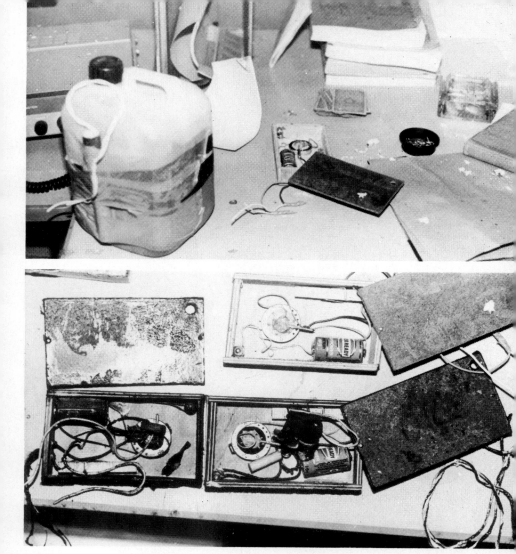

Top: A defused blast incendiary, which comprised one gallon of petrol plus high explosive. One of three found in the customs post at Newry.

Above: Three timing and power units from the incendiary devices at Newry customs post.

Right: Kevin (right) relaxes after an incident with Royal Engineers sergeant Terry Woods.

Her Majesty the Queen meets, from left to right: bomb disposal officers Major Nelson Gunson, M.B.E., G.M.; Mr. Peter Gurney M.B.E., G.M. and bar; former chief of the Metropolitan Bomb Squad and Major Kevin Callaghan G.M., Q.G.M.

wasn't going to. I felt a flood of relief that it had decided not to do its Becher's Brook bit, but instead it suddenly planted its feet and slid the last few yards .... just as the sentry was raising the bar, which caught the beast smartly under the chin. Off the bloody animal tore again, roaring through the camp, past the offices including my own (I prayed nobody was looking out of the window at the time).

At last it began to slow as we neared the stables, only for a helicopter to start up with a roar and prompt another mad, headlong rush, the remaining couple of hundred yards to its stable, where finally, it lurched to a halt, with one totally exhausted passenger.

I was still in the saddle, how, I just didn't know, but I was white-faced and knackered, limp with a combination of fear and relief. They were mad buggers these cavalrymen, as I'd thought all along! They could keep their bloody horses. Any riding I would be doing from now on would be confined to friendly little donkeys on Blackpool beach. And I was going to play it safe and stick to dealing with my booby traps!

There was still a never-ending supply of those. I found myself cataloguing the tasks as those perpetrated by "good guys" and "bad guys." Some tasks weren't as bad as others—those were down to the "good guys." They were, of course, villains all, but on a scale of difficulty they were nothing compared with some of the devices left for us by the "baddies." They were very bad indeed.

I got to the point where I began to identify the devices according to the warring factions. I found myself saying "Not another Catholic device," or "Christ! The bloody Prods are having a go back again."

I tried to avoid doing this. I considered that my job was to put life back to normal as quickly and safely as possible, no matter who was responsible. But I was becoming increasingly aware that somebody was out there and if that somebody could take me out of the game as well with his little package, that would be a bonus—perhaps a £10,000 bonus!

I applied myself to endless checking, making sure that I did not use a particular modus operandi twice or that one of my colleagues had not been to a device in the same location and set up a control point in the same place. It involved endless checking, but to me it was all in a good cause: staying alive!

For some time we had been receiving messages over the confidential phone line that if the security forces went to a particular house they would find something to their advantage. This house was not in an area that was of any interest to us whatsoever, and it was such an obvious "come on" that we would have been daft to have fallen for it. But when there was an unexplained explosion in the same building, after several attempts to get us there, it meant that we had to investigate.

There had obviously been a small explosion inside this house, but the glass from the windows was INSIDE the building, as if somebody had broken them and then set off the explosion, hoping we were stupid.

As I cautiously nosed around I could see there was a stone floor in one room leading into another with a wooden floor, the door being enticingly open. I did not like this one bit! It was an obvious trap, so as it was a derelict house I decided to do the safest thing and destroy it. There could be any amount of explosive in there, rigged in a variety of ways to greet me and I was taking no chances.

We carried only a small amount of explosive with us, so I sent for two cans of petrol, and attached a couple of pounds of explosive to each can, linked them with Cordtex and put one in the middle of the kitchen and one by the half-open door. I radioed in that there would be a "loud explosion" - and that is exactly what there was, an enormous bang that destroyed the house completely and was way out of proportion to the amount of explosive I had used. It had clearly been a booby trap with a nice welcome package concealed somewhere in the building.

But at last, it was time for me to go home! First, I had to go for my debrief at Lurgan, where I said that I had enjoyed my tour and added, facetiously, words to effect that "Any time you want any help, just give me a call!"

Oh, my big mouth! Valerie had just got used to having me back at home, when they took me at my word!

It's always a strain returning home, even though it's a relief, on both sides, that you have made it in one piece. Both of us had got into our individual routines and were just readjusting to one another again when I was called back; there was a plebiscite due and a great deal of trouble was expected, so reinforcements were needed. Valerie was NOT amused one bit.

This time I was stationed in Belfast, where I was quickly sent to the Floral Hall where somebody had left a pen in a ballot box. It is quite possible to get a detonator inside a pen, so I duly took it outside and opened it up, to find that it was a false alarm.

I was working out of Grand Central Hotel and did not feel as relaxed as I had in Omagh. There were far more teams there and my little patch was West Belfast, where I carried out fifteen tasks — one of which ended with me almost getting shot, not by the terrorists, but by our own side!

I had been tasked to deal with a cloth bag which had been dumped on a street corner. Troops patrol everywhere in the city of course, so that any object that is left lying around is immediately suspected of being a "present" for the next brick to pass that way.

A lieutenant from the Royal Horse Artillery explained at the ICP what was going on and I looked around and spotted a low garden wall that would give quite a bit of protection; I had no wheelbarrow available and reckoned that a few shots from a 12-bore shotgun would do the job nicely.

I marked the lieutenant's card for him as to the procedure and made for the wall. I had with me an escort who was a smashing lad who stuck to me like glue and was clearly determined not to let his charge out of his sight. I had to tell him to stay put and take cover with the rest of the troops while I tackled this particular number, but, thankfully, this time, he didn't do as he was told.

I had got to the wall before I realised my faithful shadow was still with me. "You daft bugger," I said "As you're here now, keep well back and keep your head down.

I fired one round, with no result and was just about to put my head up for a closer look when I was squashed beneath the weight of my escort, who had suddenly flung himself on top of me!

"Hang on Boss!" he yelled "I heard a rifle being cocked."

I froze, pinned under my protector. Christ! What the hell was going on?

Then, from across the street, we heard an English voice: "Where did that come from?"

"Did you see that?"

Realising that it was our lads in the cordon, I yelled "It's me, ATO. Over here!" and stuck my head up to identify myself.

"You daft bastard!" came the retort "Why didn't you tell us?"

There was no time to argue. "Take cover. Four more shots, "I warned. I fired four times and heard things breaking inside the bag, but there was no accompanying explosion. Now there WAS time to argue!

It was time for my "speechless with rage" act again. But before I lost my voice I managed to call the young subaltern all the names under the sun as I delivered the biggest bollocking of his young life for not informing his men what was about to happen. I reckoned that had I let loose with one more shot from the 12-bore the lads on the other side of the street would have identified the direction of the shots and would have opened up with their 7.62s — and a garden wall would not have stopped them. I had a quick-thinking and alert escort to thank for preventing a possible "own goal" with the pair of us the victims.

But my "minder" had not finished his heroics yet. I was still in the middle of bawling out the young Rupert when there was the unmistakable crack from a .22 rifle. Before it had time to register properly I found myself swung off my feet and hurled into the back of a nearby Pig, which proceeded to leave the area at great speed. My loyal bodyguard had been standing right next to me, as usual, when the shot rang out, decided his boss was in danger again and picked me up bodily, 70lb bomb suit and all, and removed me from the scene.

He was a good lad. I made him work hard during the twenty extra days I did on my "mini tour", making him scramble into some filthy, awkward places. He chunnered on to me about it, but he was never far away and after his earlier performance I was thankful for that. Wherever he is now I wish him and his well.

Poor Valerie. She had just got used to me demanding this that and the other when I had disappeared again and now I was back under her feet. When you can demand a helicopter at any time of the day or night and get one you become aware that you have an enormous amount of power and it takes time to become a "normal" human being again when you return to your loved ones.

I was headed now for the Army School of Ammunition

at Bramley to pass on, as an instructor, what I had learned. We had bought a house now, and I became a "bean stealer", living in the mess and commuting when I could, but when the school moved to Kineton we took a married quarter and let the house, an arrangement many Army families find suits them.

My tour in NI had been highly successful, but I had been swiftly brought down to earth on my return. Without thinking, I had reported for duty at Longtown in my smart, much-prized NI trousers, only to be told, via almost the first words spoken to me there: "You can't wear those here."

It was a real comedown. I was back in the real world and it took me a long time to readjust to being plain Sergeant Callaghan again, after ruling my own little empire across the water.

But I was still alive. And there was a lot to be said for that!

CHAPTER 11

I've Been To London ....

I STARED at the note pinned to the door and read it again with growing foreboding. It was brief and to the point: "Contact SATO immediately on return."
We had been away for the weekend and had just returned to the quarter we were occupying at Longtown, Cumbria, where I had been posted. It was Sunday night and bad news was the last thing I was expecting on my return—but here it was, waiting for me. Urgent summonses to appear before the Senior Ammunition Technical Officer were not given out for no reason and I was certain I was in the clag—but for what?

"Oh my God!" I though "What have I done?" While all ATOS are conscientious and reponsible and we do our jobs with safety uppermost in our minds, due largely to the nature of the material with which we are dealing, there are ways of cutting corners to speed things up without putting people in danger. I was no different from the others in this respect and there were occasionally little wrinkles I'd used that perhaps it was better that the Boss Man did not know about. Had I done anything of this kind recently? Desperately, I played back events of the last week or two in my mind as we unloaded the car.

Nothing. I could think of nothing, which made it worse as I had no chance to prepare to defend myself when I was carpeted, as I was about to be.

Oh well, there was nothing for it but to face the music, so, heart in mouth, I walked across to the sergeants' mess and phoned the Boss.

The familiar voice boomed down the line: "Ah! Sergeant Callaghan. There you are. I've been trying to get you all weekend..." I gritted my teeth ready for the worst.

"Congratulations!" he said "It will be annonced tomorrow. I have a signal here that Sergeant Callaghan has been awarded the George Medal for EOD duties in Northern Ireland!"

He must have thought he had a deaf mute at the other end of the line, but eventually I managed to say: "I beg your pardon?"

"Sergeant Callaghan." he repeated patiently, "You have been awarded the George Medal for service in Northern Ireland."

I was totally gobsmacked. Here was I expecting a bollocking for I knew not what and they were trying to pin a bloody medal on me, if I'd heard him right!

"Sir, would you say that again?" I asked, still feeling bewildered. He must have wondered who he had been entrusting EOD work to, but, patient to the last, the Boss read out the signal again. It seemed there were numerous other signals in his possession that had arrived during the wekend from well-wishers who had heard about it before I had, but it was the first inkling I had that I had been "gonged".

When I had thought about it I knew I had put in a good tour. I'd given sound advice and earned the respect of those who counted on me on my debut in the Province, but the most I thought I could realistically have expected was a GOC's Commendation.

104

I had just done my job the way I thought it should be done and now here I was facing a trip to Buckingham Palace to be presented with my medal by the Queen. It was a far cry from the day I had joined up hoping the Army would allow me to drive their big trucks!

One of the immediate and lasting benefits of being nominated for an award was the fact that I was now able to prise out of the quartermaster a new, tailored No. 2 dress uniform as of right. The one I had was off the peg and fitted where it touched.

I learned, by letter, that I was allowed to take two guests with me to the investiture, so Valerie and David were able to come too—which, needless to say, cost me a new outfit for Val.

We had to be at the Palace by a fairly early hour in the morning on the day of the investiture, so we drove down the previous day and stayed with Merv Chapman, an old service mate, who was living at Twickenham, which I thought, would be nice and handy.

Wrong! With Merv's instructions it should have been a piece of cake—and it was, until we hit the first set of roadworks, complete with diversion. As I tried to keep as near to our route as possible panic began to set in as we became more and more lost. We did not have an A to Z and I had no idea how to find my way around London, neither had Valerie and I knew that if you were not in your appointed place at Zero Hour they locked you out. It was as simple as that. Her Majesty did not wait for loyal members of her forces who could not find their way around.

In desperation I stopped the car in a posh square and hailed a pedestrian: "Excuse me, mate," I asked "But can you tell me how to get to Buckingham Palace?"

"I sure can pal," he smiled in a pure Texas drawl! "Go down here, then hang a left, hang another right. Go down

105

a big avenue called The Mall and at the end, on the right, is a big house. That's Buckingham Palace."

Trust me. Of all the people in London, here was I, a uniformed member of Her Majesty's Forces, lost in the big city and I had to pick on a bloody Yank to put me right! But I had him to thank for saving the day, for his directions were spot on and with a couple of minutes to spare we swept through the gates—last in, as it turned out.

Once inside we were quickly parted as Valerie and David joined the other families who were the "audience" and I was ushered, by a Lieutenant Colonel, to a group where I met up with Major Mike Newcombe, who was getting the OBE, and several others I knew who were getting gallantry awards.

We were segregated into groups, with one "minder" per group and our names were checked constantly against the other in which we had been told to stand in a display of high organisation designed to ensure nothing went amiss. Everybody stood around, talking nervously, closely eyeing the enormous paintings that adorned the walls, and trying to look knowledgeable.

Slowly, we shuffled along, down a series of corridors until we came to the rear of the main ballroom, where the ceremony was taking place. We passed across the rear of the seated families, who sat eyes front as the band played appropriate music. No doubt the Qeen was dishing out the awards down at the front, but we were unable to see her and shuffled ever onwards, out of the ballroom again and down the corridor on the far side, the whole process taking some two hours. Eventually, our minder briefed us in the last but one room before it was our turn to be presented.

"Walk to attention," he commanded "No saluting. The Queen may, or may not, speak to you. She WILL shake your hand. When she does that it's the end of the audience. Back off and walk out of the opposite door. Is that clear?"

What he did not say is that the Queen is softly spoken and that you have to pay sharp attention. And when it came to my turn to stand in the doorway as the next man, super-smart in my tailored No. 2 dress, complete with medal ribbons, including the one which was about to receive the George Medal, with the horde of families watching and the band playing—my mind promptly went blank.

Scared out of my wits, I stood at a podium as I had been instructed, and concentrated on the fellow in front of me. Suddenly, I was able to see the Queen for the first time and was struck by how small she was. It came as quite a surprise. Then, I saw the handshake and walked forward to attention as my name and award were announced.

My medal appeared on a cushion and was passed to the Queen, who took it and leaned forward to place it on the hook that had been attached to my ribbon for the purpose.

Then she spoke to me—and I could not make out a word!"

"Sorry Ma'am?" I said, feeling somewhat foolish.

"Whereabouts have you been working? she asked again.

"I was working out of Omagh and covered Fermanagh and Tyrone—in Northern Ireland," I added helpfully, as if she didn't know where that was.

"Are you still doing the same kind of job now?"

"No. I'm working at the Army School of Ammunition, training other operators," I replied.

"It's a very fine job that you are doing. Thank you and well done," said the Queen and with that out came the gloved hand for a quick up and down handshake.

"Thank you, Ma'am," I said and backed away and walked out, still in a daze. I was not with it at all. The occasion had really got to me. But I was rudely shaken out of my reverie as I passed into the corridor. A hand shot out and grabbed the medal and ripped it off my chest, another snatched the metal hook and threw it into a bowl along with a steadily-growing pile of hooks. My medal was shoved into a box with a piece of ribbon, the box was snapped shut, shoved in my hand and I was ushered on my way before I could say "What on earth was that?"

Before I had time to join my family I heard them playing the National Anthem. The show was over and we now found that being late may be scary, but it has its advantages at times. As Valerie had been last in, she was first out and in no time at all we were outside on the steps, the first to have our photographs taken with the award.

Behind us the other recipients formed a queue that must have taken hours to get through, but we were out in no time, to meet my parents, who had travelled down from the North to see what they could from outside the railings. The rift with my father, who had disowned me when I joined up, was long since healed and he took us out now for a slap-up meal to celebrate.

Now I had time to take it all in. I thought the Queen was absolutely marvellous for standing there for two hours or more, dishing out the awards. My family were ecstatic over mine. They didn't really realise until some time later precisely what the George Medal was awarded for, but to an ordinary family the honour, especially as it had been presented to me by Her Majesty, was more than they could have dreamed of.

When I returned to the base, my colleagues were genuinely delighted for me, which was touching. And as for me, I have always said that my medals belonged to everybody who worked for me and with me in Northern Ireland.

But Northern Ireland seemed a long way away now as we were ordered to pack up and head for Germany to join BAOR. Talk about timing, we had to leave for Munchen-Gladbach just before Christmas, which meant packing Christmas toys plus clothes bought in anticipation of a two-year stay. It was a lot of stuff to lump with us — or so we thought.

I had just bought a new Mark 3 Cortina Estate on the tax-free system and had loaded it and left it in the road outside Valerie's parents in Bramhall, Cheshire. We were really full to the gunwhales. Even Rusty, the dog was being fitted in somewhere. It was Rusty who gave us what should have been the hint that something was wrong by barking persistently, during the night, only to be told to "Shut up!" as we thought it was merely people walking by.

If only I had taken more notice of our faithful pooch ....

When I went out to the car first thing in the morning to fetch a suitcase I unlocked the boot, but could not find the case. Valerie swore she had not moved it and it was only after an increasingly desperate rummage through the back of the car that realisation dawned: the case was missing. So was quite a bit of other stuff too, and when I took a closer look at the lock I realised that I must have turned the key in it, then failed to close the lid properly, not yet being used to the vehicle.

Disaster! We called the police, but while we were waiting for them to arrive made a few inquiries of our own which led to a row of lock-up garages. Outside of one of them was an item of clothing which belonged to us, but when the police arrived they informed us that they did not have sufficient grounds to search the premises.

That was a blow, but at least we were insured. Wrong

again! This thought had comforted us somewhat during a long, tiring drive to Germany, but when we go there we had a lesson in "reading the small print" of documents. In this case it stipulated that items left in estate cars were not covered for theft. It was a disastrous end to the year for a young family trying to make their way up the ladder, but we had to put it down to experience.

There is never time to brood in the Army. I had to get on with my new job at Sennelager which consisted of an active role in the Northern Ireland Training Advisory Team. This was an invaluable set-up for regiments who were on their way to Northern Ireland, for it gave them a realistic insight into just what to expect in the unique situation in which they would be placed over there .... in fact, it was a damned sight more realistic than many of them expected.

We were a small team, bossed by a major. We gave presentations to the troops, who then had to play out highly-realistic scenarios, which were as close to the real thing as we could make them.

It was an extremely professional system and one that was vital, of course, to the well-being of the lads. About six weeks before their tour was due to begin, the NITAT team would go to their location and set up videos and stills, all relating to the area where they were to serve. Part of the presentation was down to me: I had to teach them exactly what was expected of them when confronted with a bomb, and what the ATO would have required to be done when he arrived at the scene.

There's nothing better than a loud bang to get the attention of your audience and I always set off an electronically-controlled thunderflash as I was being introduced—rather like the Demon King. It used to frighten them to death for a second or so, and I would add: "Yes, bang! But don't worry. We can prevent this happening" and hope that they listened well, which they invariably did, as their lives depended on doing so.

But even better than this set-up was Tin City. This was virtually our own film set — only better; in it we had shops, houses, streets, a supermarket, a bank, and even a pub, with real beer. There was also a sangar, as in Ireland, to house troops on observation duties.

We had our role players, who represented the local goodies and baddies, who were made up of the camp's non-combatant staff: cooks, clerks, bandsmen, whoever we could rope in.

The troops would then carry out a typical patrol and be faced with a carefully-staged incident and we would video their actions. Later, they could see where they had gone wrong in glorious detail and learn for a fact that the camera never lies!

They learned quickly as we were able to act out virtually every situation with which they were likely to be confronted—often with unexpected results. Our RPG attack, for instance, was particularly effective. I was responsible for the special effects, which, in this case, concerned the one-ton "pig" used to ferry troops in the Province. The driver, who was one of our "actors", would be equipped with a switch which was linked to a charge of thunderflash, gunpowder, and flour in a parcel attached to the rear wheel arch of the vehicle. As he drove through the streets a two-man "terrorist team" would appear with a length of pipe made up to look like an RPG launcher, which also had a small charge and some flour for effect.

The bad guys would "fire" the weapon and a second or so later the driver would throw his switch and there would be an almighty bang as the vehicle slewed across the road and the driver lurched out of the cab, the troops inside being expected to react in the way they had been taught. When we showed the video later it looked just like the real thing.

These videos were classics of their kind and gave the lads involved in them a vital insight into what could be awaiting them "across the water." But for some the realism, at times, was more than they could stand.

One poor lad for instance, got more than he bargained for when he took up position "on observation" in the Tin City sangar. Being on watch in these fortified "sentry posts" is very much part of a soldier's normal routine in the Province and we used to give the troops a highly realistic idea of what it was like to be machine gunned if the terrorists decided to attack such a position. What they did not know was that we had wired into the system five electrical circuits on a ripple switch. We had what were called "splats" — small explosive charges which were originally used to propel white phosphorus grenades from their dispensers on tanks or armoured personnel carriers. They made a noise like a bullet hitting a brick wall and were ideal for our purpose.

A "terrorist" would run out into the street, making sure the occupants of the sangar had seen him and fire five blank rounds. Almost immediately the ripple switch would be fired and there would be a "splat! splat! splat! splat! splat! in rapid succession along the wall of the sangar. But the members of one unit were not aware of just what we were able to lay on for their benefit in Tin City.

The soldier chosen to be on duty in this OP gave a perfect demonstration of the fact that while adrenalin is certainly brown, so is fear. For when the gunman opened up on him he was so unprepared for the splats that he rushed out of the sangar screaming: "They're using live rounds! They're using live rounds!"

The poor bloke was scared out of his wits. He knew full well it was a "dry' training area, which meant that nobody was allowed to use live ammunition, but the effect was so realistic that he honestly believed he was being shot at and it took some time to calm him down and convince him that all was well.

I could afford a smile at the poor lad's discomfiture, but it wasn't only the trainees who got caught up in the realism. When a patrol found something that we had left to resemble a bomb or something they thought was suspicious, we had to react accordingly to see whether the patrol concerned had acted in the correct manner and as the ATO I was one of the leading figures involved. One evening I was talking to the incident commander, a young corporal, after a "find." I was concentrating on what he was saying when suddenly a shot rang out. We hit the deck as one, to find ourselves face down in a pool of dirty water.

"You daft sod," I reproached myself ruefully. It had, of course been a blank round, fired somewhere in the distance, but instinct had taken over and the realism was still running high as I went to get to my feet, as the corporal cautioned me: "Hang on a minute ATO." He was really with it!

One of the problems of being the ATO was that I worked every day, starting at around 5.30 with a brief or de-brief and going right through until around 9.30 when the pub bomb provided the main event of the day's entertainment. And that was well worth waiting for.

Of all the incidents we staged for the trainees this was the one that left the deepest impression on them. In Tin City was a real pub, which sold beer and even had fruit machines which provided revenue which went towards the cost of our special effects. Our "civilian population" of clerks, cooks et al put on some acting that was worthy of an oscar or two for this one. It was simply outstanding, though those who were involved in it for the first time had cause a plenty not to agree with that view!

As per script a car would drive past the pub, a canister, with a fuse, would be thrown towards the door and within seconds of the car driving off, the "bomb" would explode, the door of the building would be blown off, the lights would go out and the air would fill with smoke and the screams of the "casualties."

The soldiers on patrol would then react to the blast and go in to the darkened premises with torches to find people with bits of chair leg sticking out of limbs, casualties lying face down, who, when turned over had eyes hanging out or intestines spilling out of their jackets, blood gushing from ingeniously-made up "wounds" as the victims pumped concealed rubber bulbs enthusiastically. All the special effects had been laid on skilfully, courtesy of the medics with an endless supply of fake blood and as much offal as we needed.

The effect on all but the hardest members of the patrol was memorable, to say the least. Shortly after entering the pub blokes would come out and start heaving their hearts up at the sickening sights they had witnessed.

But they had to pull themselves together, go back in and get on with it. Nauseous it was. But this was only play-acting and they knew that next time it might be for real.

CHAPTER 12

"Go South And See What You Can Do"

"DON'T mess about. Get your backsides back to Longtown. You are going to the Falklands!"
There was no arguing with the message that Dick Gill and I received that we were about to play our part in Operation Corporate in the early summer of 1982. We were in the middle of a shooting competition on the range at Fulwood, Preston, at the time and we were quite under the impression that the lads from bombs and bullets were not going to be needed to help in sorting out the Argies.

When Galtieri and his mob invaded I was part of Shadow Unit - 421 Unit, which was a mirror-image of 321 in Northern Ireland. Our role was that, in time of war, we would go to our assigned location and fit into the overall pattern in the sort of manoeuvre that the Army carries out so efficiently.

It was decided that 421 would be needed Down South and we received a charter that was short and to the point: "Go South and see what you can do." "We" comprised Captain Gill and me, by now a Warrant Officer Class 1.

We were put on seven-day standby to go, during which time we got all our specialised EOD kit together—then stood ready and waiting in our starting blocks. The thought of going to war was softened somewhat by the news that we would be going on QE2, which sounded like a very upper-crust way to sail into battle, but when the great Cunarder, with its complement of Guards and Gurkhas, sailed without our little group, we were stood down and returned to normal duties. It was a great sense of deflation at not being wanted after we had got all hyped up and our families had been filled with the apprehension of waiting for us to go off to a war in which, by this time, ships were being sunk, aircraft lost and people were being killed.

Part of "normal business" at Longtown Ammunition Depot, where I was stationed, was to take part in a shooting competition that was being held at North West HQ. Dick and I, both on the team, were half way through it, with the Argies now pushed firmly to the backs of our minds when the message was delivered that we were to report back.

"No, no, no, no!" we insisted, almost in unison "We are not going now. We're not even on seven days."

But the range liaison officer who had interrupted our bit of fun on the range was not going to be put off. He was adamant: "Get back to Longown. You ARE going!" insisted the captain.

This was a turn-up and no mistake! While Dick scurried off to tell his family, I leaped astride my motorbike and roared off to Bramhall, where mine were staying, to break the news to Valerie: "Sorry love, I'm going after all." She had hardly had time to re-adjust to this change in plan that I was zooming off up to Longtown to link up with Dick and collect our equipment before driving down to Didcot to be briefed.

What a cock-up in communications! It had apparently been decided that as our "rivals", the Royal Engineers, were going, there must be no show without Punch, so we were also tasked to join in. By now Dick and I had an array of decorations between us, so we loftily told ourselves that what they lacked in quantity they were making up in quality. That was our story and we were sticking to it!

While we were at Didcot our Brigadier told us that we were to "See what we could do," so, armed with this open-minded, fairly flexible instruction, we boarded the ferry MV Saint Edmund, which, to my relief, I discovered had had its bow doors welded shut. Our equipment was put aboard the MV Contender Bezant. We sailed out of Portsmouth to support 5 Brigade, and a right mixed bunch we were—a mobile bakery, REME Support, RAF technicians and a prisoner of war handling group. It was this latter unit that brought home to us the seriousness of the situation when we played "POW" for them and were "processed." being issued with ID cards in case we were captured, with one half supposed to be sent to the Red Cross. If that did not bring it home to us just what we could be in for, then the last will and testament forms with which we were issued certainly did! I had a fleeting thought that I hadn't joined up to go to war—but that was exactly what I had done of course. In fact, I had already played a considerable part in the ongoing "war" in Northern Ireland, though this was a far more high-profile version of it.

The mood grew steadily more sombre as we were set to taping up the ship's windows to stop glass flying around if we were hit by a bomb or missile, with the thought of the dreaded exocets at the back of all our minds, the

117

news of the attack on HMS Sheffield having struck home hard.

As the days went by we began to get to know the characteristics of our fellow passenges and I was quite taken with the approach to life of the scores of RAF personnel.

The thing about the boys in blue, was that they were excellent technicians, no doubt about that. Their modus operandi was first-class. But they gave the impression that if we had to go ashore up the beach, so to speak, the soldiers among us would have to drag them with us. They would be expecting their transport to turn up to take them to their accommodation! Good lads all, but in reality civvies in uniform!

My somewhat hidebound views on this subject were confirmed one day when I came upon a flight sergeant who was being helped below decks in a sorry state. He was near to collapsing and for a few moments I thought it was going to be a kiss of life job. As we got farther south the decks rang increasingly with the sound of running feet as the various units honed their fitness. This day it appeared that the RAF, or one of them at any rate, had decided to join in and he was now paying the price as he was made to sit down.

We were really worried about him, but when the doctor arrived and took over he began to come round a bit—with the doc looking more and more puzzled. The lads trained hard, though they did not come near killing themselves—but this bloke had. What on earth had he been doing to get in such a state?

"Well Flight," said the doctor at length "I don't understand this. Do you take exercise normally?"

The effort to reply was almost too much for the casualty, but at last he managed a reply of sorts: "Yes Sir," he gasped eventually. "What do you do?"

"I play table tennis Sir."

This was just too much for me! I fell about laughing. Exercise? If that was his idea of regular exercise and he thought it would enable him to keep up among the hardened troops, there was not much hope for him. The RAF, with their triple issue of kit, tropical, temperate and winter, to our simple combat issue, seemed to think they were on a bit of a cruise. No doubt this toughie flight sergeant would be looking for the bus when we arrived at Port Stanley. The RAF did a fine job, no doubt about it, but yes, they were civvies in uniform, NCOs and all!

Life on board ship, for us landlubbers, gradually sorted itself out. Dick and I had cabins, up at the "posh" end. Some of the lads kipped where they could on camp beds. Basically, they had put all the "chiefs" at one end and all the "indians" at the other. Fine. Until it came to lifeboat drill .... in our cabins were instructions telling us where to muster in the event of having to abandon ship. Fair enough, until they realised that as all the senior and junior ranks were segregated, roughly speaking, into the front and rear of the ship, ergo: if we had to abandon ship all the top ranks would be together in the lifeboats and the other ranks likewise. Well, this simply would not do! The lads could not be lost at sea on their own—so many of us were re-allocated stations so that we could take charge of boats full of junior ranks, so that they would at least be lost with someone senior in charge of them! It meant that no matter where you where, when an exocet hit us, we had to do our utmost to get to our posts. You could be at the other end of the ship, with it sinking beneath you and a bloody great hole in between, but you had to get there. The theory was great, but it would have meant chaos. The fact that it was done with the best of intentions was the best that could be said about it.

The ship seemed enormous at first, but God, how small it seemed after a couple of weeks! I was still finding my sea legs when the clock was turned back to the days when I used to work for my father. They asked me to be barman! I had come full circle. The ship's skipper, Captain MJ Stockman, I gathered, had wanted a dry ship, but had been overruled, so we had booze on board. Imagine so many squaddies cooped up for weeks on a ship without alcohol! So they were going to be allowed their habitual "drop", though it ws going to be strictly rationed. The lads were allowed three cans a day, from the NAAFI shop. Our bar rules also stipulated three drinks and I was responsible for the stock and the money. There was to be no profit, I was told, but I soon got that changed, pointing out that there was no leeway for breakages etc. — so I was allowed to charge a whole half a pence profit per drink. Wow, rampant profiteering! Suddenly, I was the most popular man on the ship, with the possible exception of Dick, who had been appointed paymaster. So, we had the EOD men in charge of the entire cash flow: while he doled the money out, I took it back again! It was Dick's role that led to us being asked to deal with more cash than I ever thought I would set eyes on.

The Lieutenant, who was No. 2 on the ship, asked us if we would take over the weekly accounting of the ship's float. He promised that if we would count it out in his cabin he would have a regular supply of coffee sent in. We soon found out why. His cabin was like a palace compared with ours with a bathroom, shower room and, standing in one corner of the main room, a safe. From this he took out what he announced to be £52,000. I gaped at the bundles of £500 as they were tipped on to the bed. It was like winning the pools—but the novelty soon wore off as we were set to counting it, a job that had to be done every week. No wonder we needed the supply of coffee that, true to the No. 2's word, kept arriving at regular intervals. As we counted it in bundles the pile of counted cash grew steadily in the middle of the floor. It took us all morning to get through it and the thought of a repeat performance each week was mind- blowing. But the more I thought about it the more a cunning plan formed in my mind.

When the Lieutenant returned to find the job done he was delighted, but I cut his congratulations short: "How much money is floating round the ship?" I asked.

"Oh, about £3,000-4,000," he replied.

"Then why don't we put £30,000 away in a sealed envelope that we can all sign and then we can cut the job by two thirds?"

His face lit up: "Great idea!" he grinned. So we did precisely that, ensuring that we would not have to go through that purgatory again. Army initiative had won the day, but I made myself one grim promise: if we got exoceted and there was no way of escape, I was going to go down with that safe in my arms and die a rich man!

With my early knowledge of bar work I was well versed in the workings of profit and surplus, but with just half a penny profit on every drink I was surprised to find myself with around £7 surplus at the end of my first week in charge. I assumed this would even itself out—but it didn't. There again, next time I totted up, was a similar amount. No matter how many times I checked, the result was always the same. Well, this steadily growing pot of cash was not going to go away, so just before I finished my stint and handed over the bar, I had another count up, found I had some £80 in hand — and announced that everybody in the bar had a free night.

Once again, for a while I was the most popular man on the ship. Only bloke to beat me in the popularity stakes was the captain, who, when we crossed the equator allowed double drinks rations—and a good day was had by all.

When we anchored at Ascension Island I came in for my most exciting experience of the trip so far. I had to go across to the MV Contender Bezant, which had accompanied us and on which our equipment was stored. It needed checking over, especially as we had an amount of explosive with us, so, unsuspectingly, I boarded a raiding-type craft, similar in size to those used by the Royal Marines. It was more like an inshore lifeboat, but I soon realised why they liked getting about in this way. To my disappointment, at first, the acceleration seemed only moderate, but I eyed the huge engines quizzically.

"Is this as fast as it will go?" I asked the coxswain.

"I'll show you when you come back," he replied nonchalantly.

Quite a few vehicles had moved about in the rough seas and our stuff had suffered some damage, but nothing to worry about, so reassured I rejoined the raider.

"Hang on!" said the cox. And with that he sent the craft scudding across the waves with electrifying acceleration. It bounced across the surface at what must have been 50mph with me hanging on like grim death, one second looking down at the sea as this water-borne flying saucer stood on one side, the next staring up at the sky as it tipped the other way. We arrived in no time at all. I was buffeted, soaked to the skin—and totally exhilarated. So that's what the attraction of the Royal Marines was. Now, I understood!

But the time for playing about in boats was soon put out of mind as we sailed farther south—and into the War Zone, which was brought home to us extremely effectively as we darkened ship, blacking out all windows and doors. If you stood on deck there were only the stars and the luminous glow of fish in the sea to be seen. It was really eerie. By now we had been picked up by our escort, HMS Brilliant. It was getting progressively colder, people were going on watch in full combat gear, and our air defence missile systems, blowpipes and javelins, were much in evidence, accompanied by machine guns. We had heard of the Argies trying to bomb ships in this area by rolling bombs out of the rear doors of a Hercules transport plane. They were clearly getting desperate and of course we were all mindful of the damage done to HMS Sheffield and the Atlantic Conveyor by the dreaded exocets.

In addition to our natural worries we now had to contend with the Roaring Forties. I had heard about them of course, but never imagined just what it would be like. One second the ship's screws would leave the water and the engines would scream, the next the vessel would plunge back into a trough with an almighty crash. It made eating a real adventure as we played chase with the dishes of food, frequently picking them off the floor.

At least I was not sick once and the mood lightened when we heard some good news: the Belgrano had been sunk! We thought that was great news and cheered the performance of our lads.

While we were replenished at sea by a Fleet Auxiliary vessel I saw what, to me, was one of the saddest sights of the whole trip. The helicopters that came and went with a variety of stores brought several bags of mail, all important to lads away from home, especially in time of war. But as I watched, to my dismay the downdraught from the rotor blades of one helo blew several mailbags over the side. Some poor lads would be missing out on their eagerly-awaited letters from their loved ones back home. I just hoped they had some more coming their way.

All of a sudden we were in close to the battle zone and playing a real part in the proceedings, which, we were relieved to learn, were going very much our way. The boys were right on top of the job now after the earlier losses of our ships. Once they had got ashore the lads had really got stuck in and shown them what British troops are made of. And now it was our chance to help a few of them as we pulled into an inlet and welcomed some of them on board. They were the Scots Guards, who fought so magnificently to take Mount Tumbledown. They were being brought aboard for a couple of days rest and it was our job to act as hosts to these fighting men. Willingly, we gave up our beds to let them recuperate with some beer and cigarettes while we got all their kit washed and dried for them. It was a welcome break for them after the rigours of living and fighting in the harsh climate of the Falklands and enabled us to catch up on some of the tales from the front.

These lads certainly had a good yarn or two to relate. They had been advancing up a valley when they had received an air raid warning red and before they knew it a group of the Argies' deadly ground-attack Pucaras zoomed past them at low level, but when they realised they were on their way back the troops were ready for them and put up a wall of concentrated fire into which the Argies flew, with several of their aircraft being downed, it was claimed.

This all brought it home to me just what could be waiting ashore when Dick and I were called in to do our bit, whatever that would be. We had readied ourselves for the task—but then came the glorious news: the Argies had surrendered! Well, blow me, they had jacked it before we had even got ashore! The next morning as we slowly sailed into Port William, the outer harbour of Port Stnley, we could see smoke from fires burning in the distance, where our lads had been doing their stuff. We sailed in the following day to be greeted with the sight of thousands of Argies milling around and being marched out to the airfield as POWs. Everywhere I looked there were soldiers, ours and theirs, scurrying about like ants among the little tin houses with their many-coloured roofs.

If you were not needed, you were under orders not to go ashore, not surprisingly in view of the overcrowding which could clearly be seen, but Dick went in to see what was going on, from our point of view.

It quickly became apparent that the British forces had a problem. Everywhere you looked there were huge mounds of weapons and explosives. Soon the locals would be coming back into the town in numbers after having been, to a large extent, evacuated to the country-side, or "Camp" as they called it.

It was only a matter of time before some curious child would pick up a grenade and start pulling at the pin; worse still, somebody would start to move the gear about, only to find that it had been booby-trapped, a trick at which the Argies were too proficient to leave any ordnance lying around. This later proved to be all-too- true and it was clearly time for us to go and "See what we could do" as ordered.

The romantic in me had formed a picture in my mind of going ashore with a heavily-armed party, leaping from our assault boat and rushing up the beach, while bombs and bullets were flying everywhere as they always do in the best films. But John Wayne would not have been at all impressed by my arrival, which was a leisurely affair by means of a little phut-phut boat.

Dick was already ashore, but the low-key manner of our entry to the theatre of war did not make our task any less daunting. We had no way of knowing what surprises the enemy had left lying around for us. For the fighting troops the action was over. But for us, it had just begun.

CHAPTER 13

War Is A Dirty Business ....

I F there is one thing I will remember the Argentinians for it is their personal habits. Or, to be more precise, their apparent total lack of personal hygiene.

As we began the task of organising the collection of the discarded ammunition in and around Port Stanley it quickly became evident that the Argies had left huge mounds of the stuff in every nook and cranny. The amount of ammo left in the town will stay in my mind for a long time, but what is indelibly and most unpleasantly etched in my memory is the amount of human excrement left behind by the enemy.

We all have to go, but while one of the bits of black humour to come out of the Falklands was the story of an unfortunate soldier out in the field falling headlong into an enemy latrine, in Stanley the Argentinians apparently did not bother with such basic facilities. To put it bluntly: there was shit everywhere! It was easy to spot where they had been billeted for any length of time, by the piles of human ordure they left behind. If they had been in a dugout they had simply crept into a corner and crapped! If they had paper they had left it on top of the pile. If not it was clear they had used their hands instead, then wiped them on the walls.

Such behaviour in the British Army would rightly land you on a serious charge. To anbody living in the field it is vital for the sake of avoiding disease, as well as observing the social graces, that such matters are dealt with as hygienically as the situation allows, but somebody forgot to tell these barbarians. If they wanted a crap they did it there and then and sod whoever came along after them. And in this case .... that was me! It was my task to examine all the nooks and crannies for ammo and in particular, booby traps. As some of the places they'd been living in had restricted headroom it meant I had to crawl in and the sort of booby traps these dirty sods had left behind made life very unpleasant indeed. If I did not watch where I put my hands and feet I would literally end up "in the shit!" It was here I realised another meaning of the old adage: "War is a dirty business."

I'd no inkling of this unpleasant development when I landed at Stanley pier just a short while beforehand. The only thing that was on my mind then was the amount of ammunition everywhere.

As I came ashore with my kit in black plastic bags to keep it dry, my eye had caught sight of something in the mud at my feet. I looked closer and saw several rifle bullets, so, being a good ATO and safety conscious I picked them up, carefully balancing my kit on my shoulders as I did so. But as I straightened up my eyes fell on an amazing sight that made my act of precaution look totally superfluous, for there, not 20 yards away, was the biggest heap of ammo, rifles and explosives imaginable.

I glanced farther along the street and there was a similar mound a few more yards away, then another .... and another. The beaten Argies, returning to the town, had simply dumped their equipment by platoons and left it there. I threw the bullets back into the mud and went to find my accommodation.

I had no idea where to look for the street in which Dick and I had been billeted with a local family, but thought my troubles were over as I spotted a local man.

"Where's Hebe Street?" I asked him.

"I don't know. Who lives there?" he replied.

"I don't know," I shrugged.

I'd assumed that in such a small town the locals would know all the street names. Not so. It apeared they knew where just about everybody lived, but not their exact addresses by roads. But after some bumbling about I found the little tin house and knocked on the door. The house belonged to David and Diana, the owners of the West Store and moments later, after Diana had made me take off my boots, I was sitting in the lounge, where Dick was already ensconced with David, with a glass of red wine in my hand, while the lady of the house prepared a magnificent dinner of roast beef, Yorkshire pud and two veg.

As I sat there trying to get my land legs after too long afloat I thought: "Yes, war is hell!" I was brought rudely back to reality when Dick and I retired to our room for the night. The only heating in the house came from a peat burning stove, which heated the water, but little else—and it was freezing! Quickly I got into my sleeping bag, taking off my clothes while inside, then putting them under the bag on the bed, where they would remain warm.

We woke to find the condensation on the windows frozen—and even the glass of water in which Dick had put his false teeth! Boy, was it cold! But it was a darned sight better than what the lads in the field had, where all they had to protect them from the elements were their bivouacs.

It was time to go to work. Dick had been allocated a

Mercedes 420G which the Argies had taken without paying for. They had done their best, after the surrender, to immobilise all the vehicles by smashing the ignition locks, but they had all been hot wired and, as usual, the British Army coped.

A quick tour of the area showed us that it was obvious to a blind man that the amount of armaments left lying around was enough to fight another war. It was everywhere, boxed and unboxed, primed and ready to fire, with batteries for whatever weapons needed them. And never had I seen so many varieties of rifle grenades.

We decided that the best place to move it was to the old airfield, which had access by road. It had to be moved pronto, because the locals would soon be coming back into town after taking refuge in the Camp and the thought of a kid pulling the pin on one of the all-too-plentiful grenades in the vicinity of all that ammo was too awful to contemplate.

By now we had linked up with another ATO who had come into town the hard way — across the island on the Royal Marines' famous yomp. He had a few contacts and we used his local knowledge to commandeer a flatbed truck, plus half a dozen squaddies, who we put to work loading the ordnance and driving it the couple of miles to the airfield.

Gradually the piles began to disappear. But word had got around the troops as to the whereabouts of the ammo dump, and in the time between us finishing work for the day and returning in the morning, huge piles of ammo would appear, kindly brought to us by our various units who no longer needed it!

The amount of weaponry and various bits of kit was too enormous to describe and in the end we had to station somebody on the site to monitor it as it came in in a steady stream while we dealt with the stuff left around the town by the Argies.

And there was seemingly no end to their contribution. Wherever there was a garage, or shed, barn or lean-to they had crammed it with ammo. On the old racecourse they had dug eight holes, each big enough to comfortably take a three-bedroomed house, then filled them with ammunition. These were in the process of being camouflaged, but they had reckoned without the weather, for along had come the rain and flooded every pit!

At the front of my mind all the time was the knowledge that each pile could so easily be booby-trapped. It would have been the easiest thing in the world to take the pin from a grenade, hold the fly-off lever, then place it against a wall with a heavy box of ammo against it. Then, as soon as it was moved—bang!

A great deal has been made of the Argies' alleged booby traps, but I can honestly say that we did not come across a single one—or hear of any others being found. But the amount of crap that they had left around was enough to cope with, in any case. That was deadly enough!

One of the more exciting jobs was clearing ammo from the battlefields. Staff sergeant Kevin Jolly had now joined us and he and I were touring the front lines one day when we came across anti-tank wire-guided Cobra missiles. These were fired by electric current and were guided to their target by a joystick.

These little beauties were powerful enough to take out a light tank—but they had been pointed in the opposite direction from which our lads had launched the attack!

There was no way I wanted to pick these up or blow them up where they lay—we had a better idea. Soon we had found the necessary controls and had one wired up. One good thing about the Falklands, there was no worry about ramblers suddenly appearing over the hill, so we left the rocket on the ground and fired. The projectile lifted about ten feet off the ground, then another rocket kicked in and it took off with an ear-shattering roar, tearing across the sky before plunging into the ground. Kevin looked at me. I looked at Kevin—and we rushed to wire another one up!

This was too good to be true. We fired off all six in this way. We found several dozen more, but they were still in their packages, so we left them still packed and contented ourselves with the spot of fun that had brightened our day considerably.

It was my intention to fire off every sort of weapon that the Argies had left lying around. I would never get a better chance than this. I had a go at their rifle grenades and 90mm anti-tank gun, but one thing I did chicken out of was their Sam-7 missiles, designed to bring down aircraft. I had all the necessary gubbins to fire one, but the wind was so strong the all-too frequent helicopters could appear before you heard them, and I knew if I fired a missile what was bound to happen—Murphy would take over, a helo would appear from nowhere, the missile would take off after it—and Kevin would be in the shit again, not to mention the unfortunate occupants of the chopper! I simply did not have the balls to risk this one ....

But I did fire everything else that came to hand and when the occasion called for it, carried out some spectacular demolitions. When we came across ammo that was no use to anybody we would use their explosives and our detonators and set off an explosion of up to 500lb on the spot.

But the daddy of all our big bangs came one day when we had a huge amount to dispose of. We found an area on the other side of the town where we could safely carry out a large-scale demolition and blew up nine tons of explosive in one go.

131

I got an insight into the attitude of the Argentinian senior ranks to doing hard work of any sort when one day I needed some work doing along the sea front. I had a group of POWs assigned to me. But they haughtily made it clear that they were not going to work for me: they were senior NCOs, after all. No way was I having that! Through the Military Police inerpreter who was with them I said, while pointing to my WO1 badge on my sleeve, that I was one of the most senior NCOs in the British Army and that if I was getting my hands black they could do so too. That was another battle our side won and I got a couple of days' work out of them before they were shipped back home.

That was one incident I remember with satisfaction. But there was another that gives me vastly different memories. And I see it all over again in slow motion even now when I think about it. This involved our lads this time, while they were helping me shift ammo from out of the various nooks and crannies into which the enemy had stuffed it, though it was no fault of our blokes that I ended up having one of my nastiest nightmares.

A great many places around the town were inaccessible by vehicle, but I had laid my hands on a platform trolley on which we could drag heavy loads from out of their back street hideaways.

The lads were having the usual laugh and joke while they were loading up and we had just started wheeling the trolley towards the main road when a one and a half inch hand-held rocket fell off into the road and went off.

The laughing stopped in a flash and in the twinkling of an eye the lads had dived for cover wherever they could, while I stood, transfixed, watching where it was going. From our spot in this back entry the rocket curled inexorably towards the rooftops of the tiny houses. I breathed a sigh of relief as it whooshed safely between two houses—

then, would you believe it, the only Chinook helicopter that was operational at the time appeared out of nowhere .... and of course it was right in the path of the missile!

I stood transfixed in horror as the giant beast flew across the path of the rocket—with its characteristic "wokka-wokka" noise from which it derives its nickname. The war was over, but little did the pilot know he was now under fire!

"Oh Christ no!" I thought as the missile homed in unerringly.

My luck had been in when the rocket had missed the houses, but to be so lucky twice was asking too much. I watched as the rocket hit the Chinook tail section—and bounced off.

"Oh shit!" I cursed "There goes my pension!"

Fortunately, and to my intense relief, the great beast flew on apparently unharmed, but I knew I could be in serious lumber this time.

What the hell was I to do? Did I mention it or not? While these posers raced through my brain I recovered the lads from their various hidey-holes and got the rest of the load delivered without incident, by which time I had decided to play the matter by ear.

That night, over dinner, I broached the subject casually with Dick: "Anything happen today?" I inquired innocently.

"No. Nothing." he replied

"Nothing at all?"

"No. Nothing."

"I had a one and half inch rocket hit a Chinook," I said. "Oh?" he said, surprised. "Well it was not reported."

I breathed a sight of relief and left it at that. I made a note of it in case the incident was brought up later. It never was, but it frightened the hell out of me for quite some time.

133

Life, after that went quite methodically as we toiled to get the job done. We co-operated closely with the Royal Engineers, who were extremely busy coping with items such as 1,000lb bombs that had not exploded.

Our hosts made us as comfortable as possible and were kindness itself. The system worked well, with Dick and I bringing in our rations and David and Diana sharing their wine with us.

It was as pleasant as it could be under the circumstances, but there were drawbacks. One of these concerned the bathing arrangements, which were quite horrendous. The water supply had been cut off by British shelling, which had cut the water main, with the result that we had to manhandle in our water in jerry cans and fill the cistern.

When it came to having a bath, which we needed virtually every night, we had to establish a pecking order. The lady of the house had her bath first, followed by her husband—I doubt they bathed together as that did not seem to be the Falkland Islanders' scene!—then Dick went, followed by me .... all in the same water.

When we had got ourselves clean, Dick and I then washed our combat trousers. The result of all this washing and scrubbing was half an inch of mud in the bath at the end of our ablutions, with more to come the following day as we plodded on with our task.

But at last we could pronounce our mission complete and we could go home again. It had been "different", of that there was no doubt, with the odd hairy moment, but it had been a far cry from the knife-edge tension and frequent dangers I had only just experienced on my second posting to Northern Ireland, where I had been involved in the greatest nightmare of my life ... and which resulted in a second meeting with the Queen.

CHAPTER 14

"Back Again, Mr Callaghan?"

IT was almost like coming home, I thought, as I passed through the great iron gates. Last time I had been here I had been rushed, nervous and unsure of the coming ordeal. But now, Buckingham Palace held no terrors for me. I was an old hand at Royal presentations!

To say that Northern Ireland had been eventful would be one of life's greatest understatements. It had almost cost me my life in the most horrific way, but I had survived. I had "beaten the clock." I was still one of the Queen's bomb disposal men, running around with a £10,000 price still on my head—and I was about to be decorated for my efforts.

I knew I had something coming my way after my adventures in Bandit Country across the water. I was confident I was in for a Queen's Commendation, or something of the sort, but when I learned I had been awarded the Queen's Gallantry Medal I was staggered. I have learned since that I was in line for a second gong, but there was a great deal of deliberation about me and in the end the QGM was put on the list to take the place of the GM. I learned that the man who was in charge of such matters did it because these two medals had not been issued to one person before and it would be a long time before they would be again. It was a unique "double" award and I was highly honoured again, personally and for my loyal team who had backed me so brilliantly.

I was almost a WO1 by now. I was togged out in a new tailored uniform and felt I knew the score by heart this time. As Valerie had accompanied me on my previous visit she suggested my mother and father should go with me. It is something for which I will always be grateful as it meant so much to them. Dad, who had once announced "the Queen has gained a soldier, but I have lost a son," when I joined up, had long since forgiven me. Now he was as proud as any father. We stayed at the Union Jack Club, went to see "Evita" and went off to Buck House by taxi. The old man even picked up the bill for the weekend. Brilliant!

As we were marshalled into the required order I met a colleague called Anderson who was down for the GM and was able to pass on a vital bit of inside info: "At the end, get out smartly and get your photos taken, or you'll be here hours," I warned him.

This time I was last but one in the line-up and was able to give the "new boys" who were in awe of the whole grandeur of the occasion, the benefit of my great knowledge. But I began to feel a bit less cocky when I was taken out of the line and put at the back by a Lieutenant Colonel.

"Callaghan?" he said.

"Yes"

"George Medal?"

"Er, no"

"Oh, right," he said, disappearing, with a frown. This was a bit of a shaker. Somebody had already inquired whether I was there for the GM. Surely there was no cock-up? I held my breath, but shortly he returned and to my relief said "Queen's Gallantry Medal?"

"Yes!" I said eagerly, relieved that he had it sorted out.

Having cleared up that last minute hiccup I was able to concentrate on the easy part: meeting the Queen!

This time, I remembered that the Queen is softly spoken and gave her my best attention as I stepped forward.

"Back again Mr Callaghan?" she asked. I nearly fell over with surprise! This was a friendly touch I had not expected. I realised later, of course, that she would have been briefed, but I was highly chuffed. She really made my day.

"Yes, Ma'am," I replied.

"And what for this time?"

"Bomb disposal duties again, Ma'am."

"Oh, and where were you this time?"

"Bandit Country, Ma'am."

She looked puzzled and I went on to explain: "Crossmaglen, South Armagh."

The Queen smiled at this and said: "Oh yes, and are you still doing the same job now?"

"Yes Ma'am, in England, but it's not quite as dangerous."

"Well thank you and well done," said Her Majesty and pinned on my medal.

I backed off and walked away, ready, primed this time for the man with the grasping hand I knew was waiting to ambush me just out of sight.

As I walked out into the passageway I fiddled with my medal, unhooking it ready, before the grasping hand could seize it to throw the hook in the bowl. But just as I was in the act of removing it the bloke looked me in the eye, shook his head and warned: "No."

By this time they were playing the National Anthem, so I stood there, rigidly to attention and within seconds the Queen, that nice lady who had remembered her old friend Callaghan from last time, passed just a few feet away, rewarding her hero with another of her warm smiles as she did so. It was a great moment — and it lasted a whole two seconds or so. But no sooner was she out of sight than the dreaded hand shot out and grabbed me! It snatched my medal, grabbed the hook off it, chucked it in the bowl, shoved my medal in its box, and bundled me out of the door to bring me down to earth with a bump!

This time I was able to have my photo taken with my parents, wearing both my medals. My dad was pleased as Punch and off we went for a celebration.

The black days of our relationship were long behind us now. The Queen certainly had a soldier, but the Old Man had a son again and on several occasions in the future he would embarrass me, in company, by recounting tales of what his son did.

CHAPTER 15

Cat And Mouse

TO say I was furious was the understatement of the year. A few minutes earlier I had been quietly looking forward to Christmas and New Year with my family and now I had been called in to the office to be greeted with the news: "You are being brought forward to go to Northern Ireland."

"What!" I said incredulously "Why me?"

I was due to go in February the following year and had done my pre-operational course in readiness. I knew I would have heard if anybody had been killed or injured, requiring me to take over and this was just too much.

"Somebody has been taken off the list and you are next to go," was the bland explanation that met my burst of anger.

"Who is it? Why?" I demanded to know.

They would not tell me. "He's got a domestic problem," was all they would tell me.

"Domestic problem? I'll have a bloody domestic problem if I have to tell my wife I'm going before Christmas!" I yelled back.

"But this man's wife has left him ...."

"Mine will leave me, too!" I was seething with indignation. Was I going to tell 'em!

"Ah, er, yes .... but she's left him for, er, another woman, and she's left him with the kids ...."

"What? Oh ....!"

Well, that took the wind out of my sails completely. There wasn't a great deal I could say really. Whoever the poor guy was I felt sorry for him, but I soon began to feel really sorry for myself when I found out my new area of operations. I was going to South Armagh: Bandit Country!

This was so-named for good reason. In fact, it retains that tag to this day, on ccount of the high-level of danger there and the horrific incidents down the years. It was regarded as the most dangerous place in the whole of Northern Ireland. It abuts the Border with the South and provides the terrorists with ideal escape routes, enabling them to set off their devices from across the border, or plant them and be back across it before they have even gone off — or even to shoot at soldiers from the other side.

I got an acute case of depression. Superstition was part of our folklore, where you did not go and do somebody else's task or let them do yours in case anything happened you would later regret and here I was taking over somebody else's entire series of tasks — and in Bandit Country, of all places.

This was it, I knew. St. Peter had the Big Book out and was rapidly flipping through it looking for the page with the name K. Callaghan on it in big bold type. And I knew he was getting closer to it all the time. I did not voice my fears to Valerie, but I was certain I was not going to come back this time.

But there was nothing for it but to get on with the job to the best of my ability and apply myself to outwitting the terrorists again .... and try my utmost to stop anybody collecting a nice little earner for taking me out of the game.

I was soon in the grim surroundings of Bessbrook Mill,

but cheered up when I was taken out almost immediately on a "milk run" by Gazelle helicopter on a tour of the districts, to meet the company commanders in Newtown Hamilton, Forkhill and the place where, at that time, I believe, one in six of all soldiers killed in the Province had met their fate: the notorious Crossmaglen. But they were all extremely unfriendly places and we went out complete with camouflage cream on our faces and it was a quite exciting start to my tour.

I was delighted when I found that the resident infantry battalion was the Welsh Guards. I had worked with them before. They were a fine bunch and many of them remembered me.

One of these lads, who was stationed at Bessbrook at the time, was a youngster called Simon Weston, who, some two years later, was to capture the hearts of the world with the story of his stoicism after suffering terrible burns when the Sir Galahad, the very ship which had brought them here to Ireland, was bombed at Fitzroy in the Falklands.

To my knowledge, we never met, but I did know quite a few of his fellow Guardsmen well, and I heard with horror of the tragedy that had befallen them, even as I was waiting, offshore, to land on the islands. Later, I was able to visit them in Port Stanley and found that some of the lads I knew had been among the injured.

But here, of couse, we were fighting a very different kind of war and the Guards helped me settle in. Their RSM, Mr. Constable—or "God" to his men—and I, remembered each other well, and it was a reassuring start after my earlier fears, which now receded as I got on with the job.

Just how different a posting this place was for the soldier came home to me thanks to my latest hobby. Just about everybody, it seemed, was into the latest craze of pin and string pictures, in which you fashioned your picture on a frame and wound the string, or twine around them to form your picture. This was an ideal way of passing the many boring hours between tasks as it needed concentration, but I soon needed some more pins.

I decided to get them on the way back from a trip to Lurgan. A member of the WIS (Weapons Intelligence Section) team, known to us as "Magic" because we could not pronounce his Polish name, accompanied me in an unmarked, or "Q" car during a quiet spell, in which we went to collect some stores—batteries, videos, etc. We caught up on the local gossip in the mess while we had something to eat and heard plenty to entertain us as it was such a hotbed of incidents. Then, on the way back, I decided we would call at a small village, about half way back to base, which, in those days, was designated "safe"—provided you did not go there and parade around overtly.

We pulled up outside a hardware store which was at a fork in the road which formed a triangle. We parked some 40 yards from the shop, concealed our automatic handguns and went into the shop, in which a clanging bell summoned the shopkeeper from the rear of the premises.

"Yes sorr? And what would ye be wantin'?" he inquired.

"Have you any threequarter-inch panel pins, please?" I asked in my best English accent. There was no point in attempting to disguise it, he would rumble us immediately.

"How many would ye be wantin'?"

"Oh, a good-sized box. What size boxes do they come in?"

"I don't know," he replied "I'll go an' have a look."

With that he disappeared again into the rear of the shop, while Magic and I took a look around to pass the time. And pass the time we certainly did. After a few minutes he hadn't returned. Clearly, he was making a very thorough search for those pins.

A couple more minutes passed and Magic and I glanced at each other. Obviously, we were thinking along the same lines: "He's taking a long time to find a few pins. Is he making the damned things—or what?"

It was the "Or what" that alerted me. The hairs began to stand up on the back of my neck as I began to feel distinctly uneasy. Not a word was said as Magic walked towards the door and I remained near the counter, listening intently. I could not hear a thing, no sound or somebody rummaging about searching—nothing.

It was beginning to go dusk and as I looked round, I realised that we were standing there, in a glass-fronted shop on the main street, nicely lit up and clearly visible. This may have been a "safe" village, but it was, after all, in Bandit Country. We had, in Army parlance, been in one place too long. Clearly , we were outstaying our welcome!

Magic beat me to the punch: "Come on. Let's go!" he urged.

I needed no second bidding. I was now distinctly uneasy. Stuff the panel pins!

We left quickly as the doorbell loudly signalled the tactical withdrawal of two extremely nervous soldiers!

As we headed for the car we glanced back and there, coming along the street behind us was a large car which drove slowly past the shop. It was even the archetypal black one you used to see in all the best gangster movies. Slowly, it went past the shop, three men inside it. They appeared to be taking a great interest in the inside of the building—or were we just being paranoid?

We did not stop to find out. This was no time and no place to be taking chances and we legged it back to the car as fast as our legs would carry us and were on the move before the doors were properly shut.

With a mutual "Bloody hell!" we looked at each other in naked fright as we tore off, checking to see whether we were being pursued. To our utter and intense relief, the black car had already gone down the other leg of the junction, but we raced back to put as much distance between us and it as possible.

The gates of the base opened welcomingly, with a feeling of "made it!" and we reported that we had been involved in a suspicious incident. Magic, being a member of the military police, knew the drill by heart. We did not have the car registration number, unfortunately. It's a bit difficult to notice such things when you are going hell for leather in the opposite direction! We may hve been wrong in our assumptions, but it was better to be safe than to find yourself on the receiving end of a few rounds from an Armalite rifle.

In the end, I had the panel pins sent over from England. Much safer!

True to its reputation, Crossmaglen featured a radio-controlled bomb which went off in the square, seriously injuring a soldier, who later died. It was a devastating blow and the team and I had to go out and survey the whole situation, investigating the line of sight used by the terrorists to set off their hideous device and find any clue we could that might be of future use.

There was always something different to task the mind whenever we were "on business". There were still the long periods when nothing happened, but there were more incidents in this area and I applied myself to my old maxim: "Think like a terrorist" as I did my utmost to postpone my appointment with St. Pete as he flicked through the pages ....

At least our jobs had a variety to them. A horse box

trailer was reported on the Ballymena Road. It had been stolen in the South and left some 500 metres from the Border. We flew in a Wessex and kept it under observation for several days. There were two locks on the trailer, which had a fold-down type ramp. I was not taking any chances and blew off the locks. But there was something that was not instantly apparent, until, bang! I blew off the locks, which were strong—and also the back door and most of the sides of the trailer, which weren't!

The vehicle contained some pop music equipment belonging to a group. Later, because he was so pleased to get his amplifier et al, back undamaged, the owner donated a £10 Irish note—which was worth precisely £8.63 in our money.

The keen nose of one of our highly-trained dogs caused us a rare fright while we were out on an aerial reconnaissance in the country. We were called in to a "find" by this well-meaning animal, only to find it was a hoax. But now a small team of us were on the ground with our equipment, in the middle of South Armagh .... and our helicopter had flown off. I got on the radio to summon it.

"This is Felix. Come and pick me up," I requested.

"Sorry Felix. There's nothing flying at the moment because of the weather," came the reply.

This was something we had definitely not expected. The cordon of soldiers, brave lads all, were used to walking back to base, but it was not our scene at all. Whenever people say I am brave, I always remind them that it is the troops on the ground, who patrol, who are brave. There is no way I could do their job and I did not envy them their mode of operations at all as we ran back to Forkhill. We made it safely, ducking through the little entrance door gratefully, to await better weather and our faithful helo, but I did not like it one bit and neither did the lads.

Army life, even in Bandit Country, goes on as normally

as possible, when the work is done. You'd go mad if it didn't and there was no way we'd ever let the terrorists frighten us into hiding under our beds waiting for something to happen. So an invitation to the officers' mess at Crossmaglen meant a pleasant break for me. I had been invited, as a special guest, to dinner. All I had with me was my regimental combat suit, but I put on a clean shirt and pullover for the occasion and off I went.

I did not drink a great deal in those days, and in any case, was on 24-hour duty while at XMG, but I had a glass of wine at dinner and by the time it turned 10.30 or so I knew we would not be going out that night, so had a gin and tonic and relaxed.

But where else should Murphy's Law strike, if not in Ireland? Sure enough, towards midnight the phone rang with a message for Felix: Three bombs in the Customs Office in Hill St., Newry. There had been two explosions and third was expected to go off at any time.

Thank you, Paddy. To get there it was about a seven-minute drive, but of course, we could not go the direct route as that might be just what the local banditry wanted us to do. The lads were miffed at being called out at that time, but excited at the prospect of another job. We took 40 minutes or so to get there. No way was I Brahms and Liszt, but I'd certainly had a few and it would give me the chance to clear my head properly and gather myself.

When we arrived I was ready to go and learned from a fireman that there was believed to be a bomb on the third floor. This would be impossible for Wheelbarrow and meant a manual approach. On went the suit, with my No. 2 ordered to follow one flight of stairs below me, with a fire extinguisher in case the device went off while I was up there.

Slowly, I walked down the corridor, until I spotted it on

146

a table in a room—a gallon plastic orange juice container, with the standard timing and power unit, with wires coming from the TPU going into the container.

At least it had not gone off in the hour since it was reported and if it went off now it would be extremely unlucky .... but you never knew. the lid of the TPU was slightly to one side and there were two double-core wires leading straight into the case metal charge fastened to the container. I had no doubts about this, so snipped the wires of the detonator and removed it and the charge away from the TPU. Then, I moved the lid of the TPU back a little farther. Inside these are a mechanical movement on a circular dial known as a memo park or parkway timer. When this goes off it makes a loud ratchet-type noise as it whirrs round. They are designed to slip into a pocket to remind people of certain important times—a meeting or a parking meter perhaps—and will vibrate in the pocket at the appropriate time.

The terrorists had other uses for them, now, of course and when I moved the lid it released the wire that was holding the contact of the device and it spun round with a loud whirring noise.

"Aagh!" involuntarily I let out a scream at the sound, which would normally mean a mighty bang, and for a moment my heart stopped.

Swiftly, I turned, expecting to see my No. 2 rushing in with the extinguisher to hose me down.

But he was still rushing up the stairs, shouting: "What's going on?" as I ran out shouting "No! No! No!" to stop him.

Not far behind the No. 2 was a fireman who had followed a further floor behind, worried as to what had happened. It gave me a nasty fright, but in the end I had taken a blast incendiary apart by hand, and with it gained some useful forensic evidence.

We were not so fortunate with another blast incendiary, which gutted Hogg's furniture shop before we could reach it.

But at least the weeks were passing steadily now, and I was steadily piling up a list of triumphs in the never-ending battle of wits, even though it was going to cost me a few grey hairs—if not my life.

My success rate was not lost on the lads, who, like true British soldiers, were anxious to pull my leg at every opportunity. I looked up one day as Magic put his head round the door of the team room.

"Felix, phone for you."

"Who is it?"

"It's the IRA."

"Oh yeah. And what do they want?"

"They say they wish you'd piss off!"

CHAPTER 16

News At Ten

VALERIE knew full well what my job entailed, but like a good Army wife never made a fuss. She was content to wait at home for my return, taking care of David and our daughter, Samantha, who had been born on August 18th 1974. Never once did she question the calls that came in the middle of the night—the calls I made before I went on a job, not knowing whether it would be the last one I ever made to her.

I never made an attempt to enlighten her with the details. She would have been too worried, but all that changed the day the age of video joined the Army.

Lisburn HQ had been issued with a video recorder that was of BBC standard. It was not one of those minute palm-corders that nearly everybody has these days, but it was state of the art then and the battalion photographer was like J. Arthur Rank, running round videoing everything that moved—which is how I proudly made News at 10—and later regretted that I had done so.

We had been sent to a radio-controlled task in which a lorry carrying six milk churns, which contained 100lb of explosive each, had been discovered. There was a great deal of suspicion and an element of secrecy concerning the circumstances surrounding this incident, but suffice to say that I had ordered another "Lilliput" jamming device, which was sent down from Lurgan and with which we swamped the area with jamming waves.

This hijacked truck was a bomb of enormous potential destructive power, containing, as it did, so much explosive, but not only did I proceed with the utmost caution, as I blew open the box body and cut the churns in half and got the detonators out, I had everything filmed while I was doing it.

It was a high-profile job, as we had the Belfast to Dublin railway line blocked off for several hours. That in itself was enough to attract the attention of the media and it quickly became an item of major interest.

I was too busy concentrating to notice the filming going on, but as soon as I knew there was nothing else untoward in the churns I allowed those who needed to do so to come forwrd from the cordon, including the ubiquitous "Magic" who was everywhere with his camera. He was compiling a set of information that I knew would be there next day, in apple-pie order, just as we wanted it, with his first-class black and white prints. If ever a man deserved his nickname it was this man.

I was busily sifting through the bits and pieces when I suddenly realised J. Arthur was there with his video.

"Never mind the fucking video. Get the black and whites done!" I said, getting my priorities right and not realising that the microphone was picking up my precise English enunciation, which, however, was all too apparent when we viewed it later.

Fortunately, this did not come over clearly on the newscast later, though no doubt it would have been dubbed out had it done so. But what did come across caused Valerie more distress than I could every have realised and for which I was truly contrite.

My thoughts were only of my own notoriety—albeit, paradoxically, in an anonymous form—when we heard that the film was being handed over and was being shown on the national news at home, the following night.

I had, as usual, phoned home before going out, and now, safely returned and feeling full of myself, I made my usual post-operative call.

"It was a good job," I said "And if you watch News at Ten you may see something of interest."

This she promised to do. But I later wished I had not told her.

There was "something of interest" on for her, all right. What she saw was an incident of major importance, with the main railway line blocked off, and her husband, waddling forward like a turtle on its hind legs in his bomb suit to deal with 600lb of high explosive, with all the high drama that television brought to such incidents.

It had a profound effect on my poor wife and she broke down and wept having seen for herself just exactly what I did.

Loyally, she never mentioned it until the completion of my tour, but when I realised what it had done to her, I'd wished I'd kept my big mouth shut. It had seemed like a good idea at the time.

This was a job that took thirty-six hours from start to finish because of its tricky nature and when I got back to base and the adrenalin had shut itself off I tumbled into bed at around 11 a.m. and they woke me when it was time for lunch the following day.

CHAPTER 17

The Tubes Of Death

"FELIX to the ops room! Felix to the ops room!" The familiar call came over the tannoy and sent me hurrying to the nerve centre of the base wondering what little delight they had in store for me this time.

They were certainly making the countdown to the end of my tour a lively one, that was for sure. And it seemed this one was going to be no exception as I learned that a mortar bomb had exploded near the fence of the RUC station at Newry.

This was a routine sort of occurrence, but the poor old Ops Officer appeared to think World War Three had broken out! I was not aware whether he had mastered the art of levitation or not, but he appeared to be operating somewhere near the ceiling and he pounced as he spotted me as reports were radioed in from all over the place.

"Ah, Felix!" he yelled excitedly "What I want you to do ...." I cut him short quickly: "Okay Sir. Where's the bang?"

"We haven't found it yet. Go down there and we'll tell you where it is."

This was not what I wanted to hear: "No, no. It's all right Sir," I reassured him "You find out where it is."

Sure enough, a report came in a few minutes later that the troops on the ground had found the seat of the explosion and were investigating.

"Headless chicken" was another simile that came to mind as the Ops Officer roared into action again.

"Right Felix! They've found the seat of the explosion. Off you go and see what else there is."

Thank you very much, but no thanks. This was NOT how we did it at all. Bomb disposal operators did not rush about half-cock. They followed procedure and by doing so, hopefully, they stayed alive and kept others in one piece too.

"No, no Sir," I said patiently "There's not a lot of point in me going down there yet. Let's see what else comes in."

We didn't have long to wait. The lads in the area had found the baseplate of a mortar which had caused the bang. It was some distance away, on the back of a flatbed truck, with ten mortar tubes on it, pointing in the direction of the police station.

These home-made devices are designed so that they can be positioned well away from the target and be fired remotely, over intervening buildings. They can cause devastating damage if they hit the mark. This is the type of weapon which was used in the attack on the Prime Minister's meeting of the War Cabinet at 10 Downing Street in February 1991. Luckily John Major and his colleagues escaped the blast caused by three mortar bombs, one of which landed within 50ft of its target.

They were lucky, others have not been so fortunate, but these weapons are notoriously inaccurate and deposit their deadly loads indiscriminately, a horrific likelihood in a built-up area.

But the news was enough to send my excitable friend off into orbit once more. By now, however, another interested observer had arrived quietly on the scene: the regi-

ment's "Old Man" — or Commanding Officer, the Lieutenant Colonel in charge of the famous Kosbies — or King's
Own Scottish Borderers, who had by now taken over the
area.

I stood quietly chatting to the Boss, while watched the
Ops officer doing his Command Performance. He turned
to me again:

"Ah, Felix! They have found the mortar base plate. It's
on a truck with ten mortars on it. But they don't think
they have all gone off."

"Well, how many bangs have we had?" I asked.

"Well, one, possibly two."

"And how many tubes are there?"

"Eight or ten. Ten I think."

Even my arithmetic could work this one out! "Well, it's
quite likely that they haven't all gone off!" I smiled.

"Ah, but there's been a bang by the truck."

It was customary, once mortars had been fired, for an
explosive charge to be set off at the firing point to destroy
as much evidence as possible, and it was the likely reason for this bang.

The two explosions had broken a few windows and
caused some structural damage in the area of the truck,
but there were no reports of anybody being hurt as yet.
And it was the desire to keep the situation this way that
was uppermost in my mind as our star of the show
revved up again.

"Right Felix. Are you going now?" He was determined to
rush me down there.

"No. What I want you to do Sir, is this: can you get
these areas cleared?"

I pointed to the operations map on the wall and indicated the streets I wanted clearing, covering the area in
which the mortars were generally pointing. If they went
off now they could easily go over the top of the police sta-

tion or fall short, or wide — and all our troops would now be in the area, making it as secure as possible for the civilian population.

"Right Felix!: said the Man of the Moment. Off he went to see to my request — and promptly got sidetracked.

I gave him a few minutes more. Our lads had been warned to get ready to mount up and they would be almost ready now, with the usual circuitous route prepared.

"Right Sir. Any luck with that clearance?" I asked again.

"Oh. Right Felix. What was it again?"

He really was a bright spark, this one. Patiently, I explained our needs again.

He was just about to go off into orbit again when a third voice joined in and lent its weight to the conversation.

"Ops Officer. Can you see to Felix's request please."

It was a polite request. But there was no mistaking the voice of authority as the Colonel made a timely intervention.

Superstar jumped like a startled rabbit. "Ah! yes Colonel."

It was just what I needed. He came back to earth with a bump and barked the orders into the communications room with a list of the streets I wanted cleared.

"Thanks very much Sir." Better late than never I hoped.

I turned with a wry smile to the CO: "Thanks very much Sir."

"It's all right Felix," he said knowingly "Off you go."

We wound our way around and about to the Incident Control Point and took a look at the truck. I could view it from only one vantage point and could not see a great deal. Once again my Terrorist Mind took over as though on auto-pilot: this looked tricky enough, but was it all it seemed to be? Was there something else hidden nearby? If so where? I concentrated 100 per cent, determined not to be caught out.

First thing to do was to go up in the air like my excitable friend back in the ops room, but this time in an organised manner!

"I need an aerial view of this. I need a helicopter." I said. There was a crossroads a couple of hundred yards away that was totally unobstructed and was an ideal landing site. The lads securing the area whistled a chopper up for me and in no time at all a Scout appeared as ordered, just like a taxi.

It whisked me up for a fly around. This was exactly what I needed — but the pilot was none too sure.

"What happens if it goes up now?" he inquired.

"It's all right from here," I said nonchalantly "We'll be able to dodge the bits coming down if they miss the blades going up."

He grinned as he relaxed. I had got to know most of the lads out here with the Teeny Weeny Airways — the Army Air Corps. They were a great bunch and just a short time later they were to serve with distinction in the Falklands where their derring do won them high acclaim.

I was much happier after overflying the area. There did not seem to be anything untoward — apart, of course, from those 10 mortar tubes which might exercise the old grey matter for a while!

"Right. I've got a much better idea of this now," I said as I returned to the ICP.

There had indeed, as had been thought, been an explosion on the truck, albeit a minor one. There was some charring evident and some burned wires visible on the back of the vehicle, but my main problem, clearly was the nine remaining mortars, which could spread death and destruction over a wide area were they to go off—and they still could.

It was my job to see to it that they didn't and the first priority was to get a clearer look by opening up the sides of the truck. Clad in my trusty bomb suit I waddled forward doing my turtle act once again and put a hook and line on the catches that held up the sides of the vehicle.

The idea was to open it up to see if we could locate the all-important control unit—the nifty little device that governed the firing of the missiles. All the wires could be seen disappearing into the back of the cab. It did not take a genius to surmise that this was where the timing and power unit (TPU) was lurking.

It would not be an ordinary one; there would be several clocks and relays in it to fire the mortars in a sequence instead of all at once. I was getting quite brave by this time, because I knew there had been a fire and all the wires had melted together giving a welcome degree of safety.

Even so, I could not relax my vigilance for an instant. You could never be sure the TPU did not have its own booby trap or self-destruct device—and it didn't pay to guess when the IRA were in the ring. It was common practice and they were highly devious at thinking up something new.

I peeked through the driver's window of the cab and saw what I was looking for on the passenger seat. The unit was intact and it was, in the words of the old popular song, time to "Begin the beguine."

This had nothing to do with dancing, a beguine, in our language, was a heavy object that can best be described as a square cannonball. It was a useful bit of kit and the plan was to place it on the outside of the vehicle and fire it explosively, when it would rip right through the metal and remove whatever was in its path. That, on this occasion, ws the TPU. And that was the theory. It didn't quite work out like that, as I discovered when I let rip and found that modern vehicles had shock absorbing zones. A couple of windows cracked, but when I returned to the scene of my intended triumph I found that all I had managed to do was put a neat indentation in the door. The plate was lying harmlessly on the floor having done virtually no damage at all.

Back to Square One, Kevin! The adrenalin is always going full tilt on a precarious job such as this of course, but it is vital to keep a cool head nevertheless. I had not realised at what level my own motor was running until I suddenly felt myself being picked up bodily, suit and all, then slammed down in a corner of the ICP. It was my No. 2 Phil. Good lad that he was, he had been keeping an eye on me and now he stepped in at just the right moment as he realised I had become hyper-active.

"For fuck's sake, slow down!" he snapped.

Phil was a little guy too, around the same size as me, and he had assessed the situation spot-on.

I blinked. "Yep. Right. You are absolutely right," I nodded thankfully as I took a breath and calmed down. Phil later joined the Metropolitan bomb squad, where he must have been a valuable recruit to their ranks. I certainly had cause to give thanks for his awareness and reading of a situation that day.

Now, I had a job to get on with! And when all else had failed I resorted to our faithfull "pigstick," the device with which we could destroy items such as this.

Sure enough, it smashed the TPu without further ado. Now, it just remained to remove the mortar tubes themselves. Releasing the truck's handbrake we then used a rope to pull the vehicle backwards so we had better access to it.

By this time the area's SATO—Senior Ammunition Technical Officer—had arrived on the scene. We were still not in the clear, with so much explosive still on the wagon and there was still one aspect of the job that was making us highly suspicious.

These mortars were the Mark 10 type—high-pressure gas cylinders. Normal enough. What appeared a bit dodgy was the fact that nine of them had one strip of insulating tape around them. The tenth had two strips on it. What was the reason, we puzzled as we put our heads together? The obvious conclusion we reached was that this could be the tube that was booby-trapped; just when we thought we had the job licked, this one would be set up not to go off until we pulled the tube clear, activating a hidden switch.

Again, it was no time to be taking chances. A rope was tied around the tubes and they were pulled clear remotely—and nothing happened! What the rings were for we never discovered. Perhaps a terrorist with an artistic bent liked the extra bit of decoration as a finishing touch to his handiwork, or perhaps they were adding a spot more mischief in keeping us guessing. They did that all right, but all was well that ended well and the following day I saw the tubes going off to a council tip to be destroyed. Another would-be atrocity averted. Lives saved, property spared. It made me feel I'd done something really worthwhile.

The occupants of the police station had been lucky this day. Of that there was no doubt and I was happy to have helped keep them safe. Five years later, however, they were not so lucky. Their station must have been a prime target for the IRA tried again with a similar attack and this time nine police officers were killed when a mortar hit its target. How glad I was that I was not there by then to witness such tragedy.

I was almost home and dry now .... but not quite. Not just yet.

CHAPTER 18

"Come Into My Parlour ...."

I EYED the plate of curry and rice eagerly. It was my favourite meal and I prepared to dig in while I idly watched television.

This was certainly a place that could give you square eyes. We'd watch anything that was going—videos, home movies, blue films or even, as in this case, children's TV programmes. It was one of the few ways of countering the relentless gnawing boredom between tasks, waiting, ever waiting, while the resident terrorist branch thought up something new to keep us occupied.

Now, my two assistant NCOs were out in the mill yard, practising, for the umpteenth time, with their kit, while I kept one eye on my food, one on the TV—and dreamed of going home. I had got to within five days of that magic date when I could leave this place on the completion of my second four-month tour. I would not be sorry to leave, but at least, despite all the obstacles that had been put in the way, I had survived ... if I could just get through the next few days, that was.

As I looked around the accommodation that was "home" to us inside the mill I thought what a pity it was that Hogg's furniture store had gone up in flames just before we could get to it a few days earlier, a victim of yet another incendiary device.

It was an unspoken agreement that every unit tried to leave the accommodation in a better state for the replacement team that it had been in when they took over. How we could have used a new carpet from that shop! The hundreds of pairs of boots that had tramped over this one were beginning to leave their mark.

Anyway, in five days it would be somebody else's problem and I did have this major project to deal with: tea, the highlight of the working day. But I had no sooner begun to dig in when the peace was shattered by the ringing of the phone. It was answered by one of the lads and my heart sank as he shouted:

"Boss! You're wanted in the ops room."

"Here we go," I thought. We were due for another job.

The greeting I received as I entered the operations room shook off any vestiges of thoughts of tea and home improvements.

"Ah, Felix. Just to let you know that a tanker has been hijacked on the main road just north of the Border."

Aha! A spot of action forthcoming very soon, I thought, so leaving the lads in the ops room to sort out the details, I hurried off to get some food inside me.

I'd got half way through my meal when a note of urgency sounded over the tannoy: "Felix to the ops room NOW!"

The information this time was clearer: two vehicles had been hijacked near the Border and the drivers were being brought in for questioning.

Several vehicles, which we later discovered numbered no fewer than 30, had been hijacked around the Province and there was a mounting air of excitement at the news that we had landed a prime target, a tanker, in our Tactical Area of Responsibility.

The two tanker drivers, Messrs. Lutton and Logan, were soon being questioned minutely, Mr. Lutton, as the driver of the tanker, soon emerging as the man with the most interesting tale to tell.

Two cars, a Mazda and a Volkswagen Golf, had forced him to the side of the road as he was returning to his base after delivering white spirit. Six masked and armed men had jumped out of the Mazda and forced him to manoeuvre his vehicle at an angle across the road, then, ordering him out, one of them had climbed into the cab and left a gallon can of petrol there.

While this was going on, two other members of the gang had waited in the Golf in front of the tanker, probably as the getaway vehicle in case of emergency, though how they would have squeezed eight of them into a Golf I couldn't imagine!

The second man had been made to park his lorry to block the main Dublin North road.

Lutton, a middle-aged Irishman, told me all he could. He had even had the presence of mind to take the registration number of one of the cars, but the thing for me to do was to have a look for myself. The road was now blocked and the King's Own Scottish Border Regiment had sealed off the Border.

Collecting my flak jacket on the way out, I shouted to the team that I was off in the Colonel's Scout helicopter to do a recce of the scene of the incident.

Normally, this was one of the highlights of the job for me. I loved flying in helicopters, but in this case, we were no sooner up than we were over the area. No time this time, to enjoy the view.

The pilot inquired how close we could get. I said that if the bomb went off, which was always a possibility, there would be an uplift of air at high velocity, with some fragments.

"What happens to a helicopter if it's subjected to forces like that?" I asked.

His reply was matter-of-fact: "It would probably rip the rotors off and there would be a downdraught of helicopter very quickly."

Charming! And thank you for the information.

"Oh well, we'll keep our distance then," I said helpfully.

I needed some photographs so that I could brief my team and let everyone know exactly what the situation was at the incident site. As we circled and the object of our attention remained in one piece, we gradually got braver and I leaned out, snapping away. But the photographs were not all that was occupying my mind.

I could not get rid of the uneasy feeling about the fact that the terrorists had made Mr. Lutton move his vehicle a few more yards into position until they had it just to their liking. What had they been up to, I wondered for the umpteenth time? They had made him leave it three or four yards from a telegraph pole, which could have been significant. There was a Michelin advertising hoarding close by and this could well have been used as an aiming point. A terrorist could lie concealed some distance away, waiting until a vehicle was lured into the area, then setting off a larger hidden device when it reached a certain, predetermined point. This was very much uppermost in my mind, along with the blast at Warrenpoint the previous year when the Parachute Regiment had been caught in similar fashion, with grievous loss of life.

I was determined we were not going to be lured into a similar trap. Carefully, I scrutinised the edges of the vehicles, trying to see if there were any wires running away towards the hedges. The terrorists could have planted a landmine nearby some time earlier and be waiting for somebody to approach that point before firing it from several hundred yards away.

I gave it every ounce of concentration as we played out the deadly game. But I could see nothing significant and used up my roll of film before returning to base, where I handed it over to the weapons intelligence section. These were a smashing group of lads, mostly from the intelligence services and military police. They were the ones who kept track of what was going on in the area, and the various trends—for instance whether a particular type of incident had occurred before. All vital pieces of information in the jigsaw.

We got on well with them and who should it be who took my roll of film to develop but the every dependable Magic. I reported back to the ops room again, then brought my team up to speed on the situation.

There was a message waiting for me from the Colonel. He was out and about, but would be joining us later. I realised that he was out dealing with some hijacked vehicles that we had earlier seen on the TV news. It had clearly been a busy day for the Chief Ammunition Technical Officer.

It was now about 5.45 p.m. and we had packed a great deal of action into the hour or so since the call had come in. And there was no rest for the wicked as there came another summons to the ops room!

The ops officer informed me that it was required that the site would be cleared tomorrow and asked me to plan on an early start. There was insufficient time for us to tackle it during the remaining hours of daylight and the area would remain sealed off, with covert surveillance maintained on the vehicles during the night until we could get at them the next day.

By this time the two drivers had been checked through the system and, as far as was known, they had no political leanings towards any organisation. It was believed that what they told us could be accepted as correct as they knew it.

That was fine—a big help as I prepared for the morrow ...and yet ... there was still something nagging at the back of my mind about Lutton's vehicle, so I went to have a word with him for the third time.

Logan's lorry seemed, from the reports, to have been very quickly dealt with. The can had been placed in the cab by the terrorists perfunctorily, but then they had taken a petrol can to the other vehicle with obvious care, holding it by the handle, and placing it, he thought, on the bunk bed behind the seats.

I concentrated hard on this one. Again I went over the diagram he had drawn for me of the layout of the cab, trying to discover whether he had forgotten any details at all. And sure enough, this time he added in another item: he remembered that his old, army-type canvas rucksack was also on the bunk behind the passenger seat.

It might have seemed an innocuous detail to my patient friend, as I got him to draw it on his diagram and to describe it in the minutest detail. But there must be no mistake when I had to take a look at it—or view it through the eyes of the camera on our remote controlled wheelbarrow the next day.

It would be highly embarrassing to "defuse" some ham sandwiches, then to find the bomb still waiting there for me when I climbed into the cab thinking all was well!

I'd no doubt that by now the driver must have thought me a nit-picking so-and-so as I pestered him for the tiniest details: how did he get into his cab? How high was the door handle from the ground? Being a short fella, I had to know whether I could reach it easily in my heavy bomb suit, or whether I needed a box to stand on. Where were the grab handles? How did the door open? Was it a tight door?

These questions must have seemed pointless to poor old Lutton, but they were vital to me and again I would look a right prawn if I got to the scene of the action all ready to go to work only to find that the damned tanker door was locked.

He was a very patient man that night was Mr. Lutton, but at last he was allowed to go home, leaving his tanker behind and a steadily-increasing flow of adrenalin coursing through me as I prepared to deal with it.

Our game plan was simply to select the right kit to tackle the job, removing petrol can and bomb, if any, leaving the tanker intact — and me with it!

Simple enough? Let us hope so. But practice, as they say, makes perfect and while I ran my eye over the photographs Magic had developed, my assistants were out in the yard yet again with the equipment. You are lucky in Northern Ireland in that you have two assistants attached to you as a bomb disposal operator and mine, a sergeant and a corporal, got to work experimenting with our faithful, ubiquitous wheelbarrow in various modes, knowing that they had to be able to get a television camera into the cab from the ground, or at least be able to see into the vehicle.

I am no Lord Lichfield when it comes to taking photographs, but the ones I had before me now provided a clear view of the area — enough from which to do our planning.

By now the Colonel had arrived and after getting the lads together for a briefing, the CATO and I went off to my quarters for what was a very important little natter.

Now, there is, as I've explained, one unwritten, yet inviolable rule among EOD operators: you do not, EVER poach anybody else's bomb task — and they never poach yours. If you stuck to your own job you did not end up with somebody else's death on your conscience.

Which left me with that all-important question for CATO:

"Colonel, am I doing this job, or are you?"

"Mr. Callaghan, it's yours," he said, which was fine and let me know exactly where I stood. Now I could get down to some serious planning.

We spent some time talking about events throughout the Province that day, which had turned out to be what we called a Disruption Day. Thirty vehicles had been hijacked and left where they would cause the maximum inconvenience. Tweny nine had been cleared by my colleagues in various areas, with nothing harmful found in them.

That left No. 30: mine. It was natural to assume that mine was part of the disruption too, and I was quite happy to think of it as another hoax, But .... hoax or not, you go through the motions and you sweat the same sweat until you have taken the "device" apart — real, or otherwise.

The Colonel left after we had put the final touches to our plan and I spent the evening with one eye on another video while going over the plan in my mind.

My assistants, the worthy sergeant and trusty corporal? Why, they were out in the yard, of course, practising with their good old friend, Wheelbarrow, making sure it was in the best possible working order for its big day!

I phoned home that evening, but did not mention the job in hand. Plenty of time for that later. The lads called me out to have a look at their friend, which looked like a praying mantis lying on its back with various bits and pieces sticking up in the air. They were happy with it and so was I, so at last they put it away for the night.

Now, there was nothing to do but wait .... and it is the waiting that is the worst part. Knowing that you have a job on in the morning makes the mind race and take you over the ground again and again in a "have I forgotten something?" routine. But at least we could go to bed, if only to snatch a couple of hours shut-eye as the tension built up remorselessly.

I was up next morning before my alarm summoned me, to find that the team had beaten me to it. They were ready to go, with everything checked and even the engines of the vehicles running, although we were not due out for a couple of hours.

A keen crew indeed! I could not have asked for better. We hadn't even had breakfast yet, but once the adrenalin starts pumping it is difficult to stop it, even though, at this stage, I was convinced that it was the remnants of yesterday's Disruption Day and I was going out to deal with a hoax.

Before leading the team off I overflew the area again in the helicopter, just for one more look — but it looked exactly the same.

Almost time to go ... and time for a quick call home as was my never-failing habit before a job. Harmless chit-chat to Val, somewhat mundane, but very important to her as she related the various goings on her end. She asked me what was going on and I said: "Nothing special." The usual white lie. Or, in this case, a bloody big black one!

Suddenly, it was time to go, at last. Out and into the vehicles. Let the lads in the sangar at the gate of the Mill know we are coming and take off with engines revving hard. This was a vital part of our routine. As soon as the troops in the sangar heard we were coming, the doors would be opened and we would roar straight out and on to our agreed route, albeit a circuitous one, going several miles out of our way to Newry, varying our route once again—all in an effort to outwit any smart Alec—or

Paddy—who might be planning a reception with one of those rather anti-social RPGs.

This was more like it: a beautiful sunny Irish day. No mist. Lovely. Everything was planned to the minutest detail—round the houses to the incident, the electronic counter-measures going on as we approached to jam any bid to welcome us with the detonation of a remote-controlled device.

Now was the hour of glory for our beloved Wheelbarrow. It was swiftly set up in the required mode and our lads had practised with it so many times it was a wonder it did not know what to do on its own, without the aid of instructions from the control panel, from which the sergeant sent it off down the road towards the tanker.

We remained in what cover we could, behind our armoured vehicles and shielded by our ring of steel provided by the Borderers, knowing full well that although there would be scant chance of a crowd forming out in the country, somewhere there would be a pair of eyes watching us, probably from the high ground, as the opposition carefully noted everything that we did and what occurred.

I had realised that it was going to be difficult to get at the driver's cab with our versatile machine, as the cab was right next to a drainage ditch. CATO arrived as Wheelbarrow trundled the 150 yards to its objective and, sure enough, just as I brought him up to date, crash! Wheelbarrow fell in an untidy heap into the ditch as the sergeant attempted to manoeuvre it. All that planning—and there it was, lying on its back like a stranded tortoise.

Now there was only one thing for it. "Suit!" I snapped and stood with my arms flung wide.

This was the signal for my lads to dress me in my five-piece armoured suit, which makes the wearer look like something out of the Tales of King Arthur.

At some 70-plus pounds the weight of the damned thing must have been similar to his knights' working clothes too. It was about half my bodyweight, in fact, which I now had to carry on The Lonely Walk, that long trudge to the target with everybody watching you, while you know that you, and only you, can deal with what lies in store for you at the other end.

But this was a high-profile situation and I didn't mind at all. The Media had arrived at the outer cordon and here I was doing a tanker: absolutely great! Normally, these vehicles were something you saw on the news or heard about when somebody else got one in his area. I had taught at the Army School of EOD the various ways of tackling them, but to be actually given one for real—even though I knew it was only a hoax—was quite a coup; a rare prize indeed.

My first task, however, was to neutralise our poor old wheelbarrow, which had loaded weapons on it and I leaned over and switched it off to end its embarrassment.

Now, to the interesting bit, I thought. I opened the cab door and hauled myself inside, taking my various bits and pieces with me.

My pulse began to quicken as I looked across the cab and eyed the device. The visor of my helmet was beginning to mist up and I gave thanks for my contact lenses. If I take off my glasses it is like switching off the light, I am so short-sighted, and Her Majesty had paid for my contact lenses to enable me to do my job unhindered.

I wedged myself between the steering wheel and the driver's seat and looked at the can. I stared at it and there was something about it that was not quite right .... I thought: "This is an elaborate hoax ...."

I could see the body of a Mark Six mortar bomb with wires coming from it, leading to a timing and power unit at the top.

And then, to my horror—I saw the mercury tilt switch! It was isoponed to the top of the timing and power unit and the wires from it were coming down to the home-made detonator, which was inside the mortar bomb body, with, of course, the gallon can of petrol as part of the set-up.

For one horrific second I thought I was about to die. I fully expected to see the Big White Light, as we call it. But I blinked and a heartbeat later, nothing had changed. I was still there, all in one piece!

Then the hairs stood up on the back of my neck as I saw the mercury moving about with my breathing. I froze as I realised the device would be activated if the liquid moved perhaps three eighths of an inch and touched the contacts.

But, I stopped to listen, puzzled. I could not under-stand what the noise was. Then, I realised: I could hear my heart pounding away with fright!

The desire to run—if I could have done so in my suit—was enormous. Desperately, I fought it back, telling my-self: "You're still here. Don't panic."

If I had rushed I would have upset the tilt switch, which was on the foam bed. I was kneeling on the seat, no more than fifteen inches from a blast incendiary with a cunning booby trap and I thought:

"My God. Somebody is trying to kill me!"

When I considered it later, it was obvious that the ter-rorists would know that I was the person who would be called out to a device in that area, although, out of court-esy, I had asked the boss if it was definitely "my" job, I had known full well that he wouldn't breach our unwrit-ten rules of "poaching." The terrorists watch our every move, know how long our tours of duty are and would have worked out that I was due to go home shortly. No doubt the fact that I had had a successful tour made me a prime target.

So there was no doubt in my mind: it had been meant for me. And St Peter had almost reached my page.

Had it gone off, the fact that I was wearing my bomb suit would not have saved my life. There is enough protection in a suit to shield you during your walk to or from a device, but there is no way you could survive a blast at that range. What a suit will do in all but the biggest blasts, is keep enough bits together to leave something to stick in a box to bury.

Now, as I kept absolutely still, I realised that the normal sounds were coming back—the sounds of silence. My heartbeat had faded in my ears as my immediate terror subsided and it was time to set about disrupting the bomb.

The long, scaffolding-like tube which comprised the disrupter, was going to be difficult to position, to enable me to leave it aimed precisely and fire it by remote control. I could have blasted off the bottom of the can, but the switch would still have worked, so the TPU had to be taken off.

The only other thing in the cab, I knew, was the driver's lunch bag. And perhaps it was going to have some use after all! The difficulty was that it was just out of reach in the far corner of the bunk. I had to reach across to it, which I did with the utmost care, keeping an eye on the mercury, which came within three inches of my face as I leaned forward.

But at last I managed to reach it. Carefully, I positioned it, leaned the disrupter against it—only for the tube to fall off. I tried again, with the same result. Then, I had the notion that if I wound the firing cable around the bag it would hold the weapon in place. I tried it—and to my relief it worked.

Now to make my escape and disappoint another bunch of terrorists. Making sure I did not foul the cable on the way out, I made the most careful tactical withdrawal in history, with my eyes glued to the tilt switch.

I got out of that cabin a damned sight more slowly than I had got into it and the feel of the ground at last beneath my feet was simply wonderful!

So far, so good. But as I waddled back to the control point as fast as I could, I saw CATO hastening towards me and waved frantically to warn him off. As we met, he shoved up my visor and I yelled: "It's real!" which was all the encouragement he needed to join me in a rush for the control point.

I told the Control Point Commander that in two minutes there would be a small bang, and if I was unlucky this would be followed by a bloody big bang and would he warn his men to keep their heads down.

While we waited the buzz went round that we'd got a real device. My team thought it was great! Their boss had expected to deal with an empty can and had ended up with a real frightener. Thanks boys!

I gave the firing signal, set it off and there was an audible crack from the cab. We peered out from the safety of our Saracen armoured cars and the vehicle was still there.

But my job was still not over. I had to go in again to make sure all was well. This time, as I approached, there was a lovely smell of petrol. As I climbed into the cab: nothing. The bomb had been smashed all over the place. A complete separation. Was I chuffed!

I checked the vehicle's tanks, but they were clear of any further "presents" and when the Boss and I had a look at the nearby container lorry it turned out to be nothing more sinister than an empty can left on the spare wheel.

So, at last I could get out of my suit and a tremendous

weight was lifted from me physically and metaphorically as I did so. It was all over and I felt really good, yet, when I found time to reflect, I realised I had learned an invaluable lesson.

I had fallen into the trap of assuming the tanker to be a hoax before I went out. It dawned on me now just how lucky I had been and that my call to Valerie before we went could have been my last. It made my heart race again, but the fact that I now had a tanker to my credit made up for the scare—even if somebody was out to kill me.

I put in another call home later that day, when the rush of adrenalin had eased off.

"Anything happening?" asked Valerie.

"Nothing special," I lied.

There was no way I could tell her that somebody had tried to get me. My relief operator was not due until the following day and I wished he had been able to be there that day. It would have been an ideal eye-opener for him.

But at last, at long last, it was time to go home, to my family and safety. I had successfully dealt with everything that the terrorists had come up with; I knew I could feel satisfied that I had done my job well. I had learned a great deal that I would be able to pass on to others in the future to help them cope when it came to their turn to face the music in this treacherous place. And, most important of all, I had survived, despite my earlier misgivings. I had made it to the end of another tour, though, my God, it had been a close-run thing.

I was all too well aware of this as I waited for the car to take me to the ferry home. I heaved a deep sigh, got out my diary and made one last entry:

"K. Callaghan went home a wiser man".

GLOSSARY

APC	Armoured Personnel Carrier
AT	Ammunition Technician
ATO	Ammunition Technical Officer
BAOR	British Army of the Rhine
Beguine	An explosively-propelled cannonball for opening vehicles
Big White Light	The explosion that will kill an EOD operator, who sees the flash, but does not hear it
CATO	Chief Ammunition Technical Officer
CO	Commanding Officer
CO-OP	Home-made high explosive
Cordtex	Proprietary name for a type of detonating cord
Come-on	A device to lure troops into an area
EOD	Explosive Ordnance Disposal
Flatsword	An explosive device for cutting open metal containers
Felix	Nickname for Bomb Disposal Operator, after the cartoon cat that kept on walking
Ferret	An Army scout car
Gelamex	Commercial explosive with a Nitroglycerine base
IRA	Irish Republican Army
ICP	Incident Control Point
Long Walk	The lonely approach a Bomb Disposal Officer makes to a device
OC	Officer Commanding
PIG	Armoured Personnel Carrier
Q car	An umarked military car
RAOC	Royal Army Ordnance Corps
REME	Royal Electrical and Mechanical Engineers
RLC	Royal Logistic Corps
RPG	Rocket-propelled grenade
R&R	Rest and Recuperation
RSM	Regimental Sergeant Major
RUC	Royal Ulster Constabulary
SAM-7	Surface-to-air missile
SATO	Senior Ammunition Technical Officer
SLR	Self-loading rifle
Tin City	A mock-up city complex in which troops train for service in Northern Ireland
TPU	Timing and Power Unit
UDR	Ulster Defence Regiment
VCP	Vehicle Check Point
Wheelbarrow	The bomb team's remote-controlled machine for tackling explosive devices